TOP REAL ESTATE STRATEGIES

Top Real Estate Strategies

CARMEN WILDE

Contents

Introduction

Overview of the Real Estate Landscape
The real estate industry is a world of vast opportunities, evolving markets, and dynamic challenges that draw in people from all walks of life. Yet, navigating this field isn't easy. With changing economic landscapes, shifting demands, and the rapid pace of technological advancement, real estate professionals must remain adaptable, strategic, and informed to thrive. In this book, **Top Real Estate Strategies: Insights from 100 Industry Leaders**, I, Carmen Wilde, aim to provide a roadmap—a collection of insights gathered from the experiences and expertise of some of the most accomplished leaders in the field.

My journey into real estate began much like many others: with an interest in creating a secure future through investments. But as I navigated the ups and downs of my own career, I found myself fascinated by the diverse approaches successful real estate professionals took to overcome obstacles and reach their goals. Each path was unique, shaped by distinct backgrounds, values, and circumstances. Over time, I saw a common theme—success in real estate is rarely achieved through a single strategy. Instead, it's the culmination of various practices, perspectives, and hard-earned lessons.

In speaking with these industry leaders, from investors and developers to agents and property managers, I realized the immense value their insights could bring to others. This book was born out of my desire to share these insights with you. It is a compilation of strategies, real-life stories, and practical advice—each contributing a piece to the larger puzzle of what it means to excel in real estate.

Purpose of the Book

The purpose of **Top Real Estate Strategies: Insights from 100 Industry Leaders** is simple: to empower you with actionable strategies and real-world knowledge. Whether you are just starting your journey or are already established in the industry, this book serves as a guide to inspire, educate, and motivate you to reach new heights.

Within these pages, you'll find chapters dedicated to essential aspects of real estate, from understanding market cycles and mastering negotiations to exploring the latest technology trends and strategies for sustainable building. Each chapter draws from the expertise of industry leaders, weaving their experiences and best practices into a tapestry of advice that's as diverse as it is valuable.

Real estate is more than just property and transactions; it's a field deeply rooted in relationships, vision, and strategy. The strategies shared in this book are not simply theoretical; they have been tested and proven in real-world scenarios. These leaders have weathered market downturns, taken calculated risks, and navigated both triumphs and setbacks. Their stories provide more than just tactics—they offer lessons in resilience, creativity, and strategic thinking.

As you turn these pages, remember that real estate is a journey, not a destination. The strategies shared here are intended to serve as a foundation on which you can build your own path. Take the insights that resonate with you, adapt them to your own circumstances, and forge a journey that is uniquely yours. I hope this book will not only provide you with the tools you need but will also inspire you to envision what's possible.

Welcome to **Top Real Estate Strategies: Insights from 100 Industry Leaders**. I'm thrilled to have you along for the journey.

Chapter 1

Chapter 1: Market Fundamentals

Understanding Key Market Concepts

The real estate market, like any other, is governed by a range of factors, but its fundamentals—supply and demand, property types, and location—are the bedrock of any investment decision. To navigate this market successfully, you must first understand how these key elements interact to influence value and predict trends.

Supply and Demand Dynamics

The principle of supply and demand is central to understanding real estate markets. When demand for property in a specific area outstrips supply, prices tend to rise. Conversely, when there's an abundance of properties and fewer buyers, prices often decrease. This simple dynamic can be affected by numerous factors, including population growth, employment rates, and economic policies. For example, a surge in a city's population due to new job opportunities can increase housing demand, while economic downturns can reduce the purchasing power of potential buyers, shifting the market toward a buyer's market.

Industry leader Sarah Thompson, a seasoned real estate investor, explains, "In my experience, understanding supply and demand in any given market is one of the first steps to determining potential property values. Even a quick look at the ratio of available properties to recent sales gives a snapshot of whether a market is leaning toward buyers or sellers."

Types of Real Estate Markets

The state of a real estate market—whether it's a buyer's market, a seller's market, or balanced—plays a crucial role in determining your strategy. In a seller's market, where demand outstrips supply, properties typically sell quickly and at higher prices. Buyers may need to act fast, often foregoing some of the due diligence they might perform in a slower market. In contrast, a buyer's market, where there's an abundance of properties for sale, allows buyers to negotiate more favorably, often securing properties below asking price.

Understanding the type of market you're in can save both time and resources. Seller-oriented strategies include pricing properties competitively and preparing for multiple offers, while buyers can benefit by negotiating contingencies or offering lower bids in buyer's markets.

The Role of Location

Location is perhaps the most well-known element influencing real estate value, and for good reason. Different neighborhoods and regions have unique appeal based on factors like school quality, crime rates, accessibility to transportation, and proximity to amenities. A property in a highly desirable area, even if it's in need of extensive repairs, often retains more value than a similar property in a less favorable location. The common real estate adage "location, location, location" highlights how crucial it is in determining long-term value.

According to Mike Chen, a veteran real estate developer, "You can change almost anything about a property—its appearance, its condition—but you can't change its location. Investing in up-

and-coming neighborhoods or those with strong amenities can yield exceptional returns over time."

The Interplay of Key Concepts

Supply, demand, market type, and location don't act in isolation—they work in concert to influence real estate markets. For instance, a high-demand location may also be a seller's market, making it challenging for buyers but advantageous for those looking to sell. Conversely, a lower-demand location in a buyer's market might offer better entry points for long-term investors, especially if the area is expected to grow or improve in the future.

These market fundamentals lay the groundwork for deeper insights into the real estate field, shaping investment strategies and guiding decision-making. By grasping the dynamics of supply and demand, understanding market types, and recognizing the critical role of location, you'll be better equipped to analyze any property's potential and respond with confidence, whether the market is booming or facing a downturn.

Economic Indicators and Their Impact on Real Estate

Real estate doesn't operate in a vacuum. It's deeply intertwined with the broader economy, with economic indicators like interest rates, inflation, and employment rates directly impacting market health, buyer behavior, and investment opportunities. Understanding these indicators provides a valuable context for making informed decisions in real estate, enabling investors to anticipate market shifts and strategize accordingly.

Interest Rates and Their Influence

Interest rates are a critical factor in the real estate market. When rates are low, borrowing becomes more affordable, making it easier for buyers to secure loans and encouraging property purchases. This increased demand can drive property values higher, creating a more competitive, seller-friendly market. Conversely, when interest rates rise, borrowing costs increase, leading to fewer buyers and often causing property values to stabilize or even drop.

High-profile investor James Whitman shares his perspective on interest rates: "I remember when rates dropped to historic lows in the early 2020s. It opened the floodgates for first-time buyers and seasoned investors alike, and property values skyrocketed. But when those rates eventually started to climb, I adjusted my strategy to focus on rental properties and value-oriented acquisitions, preparing for a shift toward a buyer's market."

Understanding how interest rates affect buying power and demand helps real estate professionals and investors time their decisions wisely. Those planning to buy or refinance properties should watch for rate changes that could impact their ability to secure favorable financing terms. Additionally, sellers might adjust their expectations if higher interest rates begin to slow buyer interest.

Inflation and Real Estate Value

Inflation—the rate at which the general level of prices for goods and services rises—also has significant implications for real estate. When inflation is high, the cost of goods, services, and materials rises, impacting construction costs and the overall value of properties. In many cases, real estate can serve as a hedge against inflation because property values tend to rise along with general price levels. However, inflation can also reduce buyers' purchasing power, potentially cooling demand in certain segments of the market.

For investors, high inflation may signal a time to hold on to existing properties, as rising property values can protect wealth. It's also a good time to consider rental properties, as rents often increase in inflationary periods. Builder and developer Rachel Gomez explains, "During inflationary periods, I've seen rental properties perform remarkably well. Rent prices tend to adjust more quickly than sales prices, so my rental portfolio provides a solid income stream that keeps pace with inflation."

By tracking inflation trends, real estate professionals can anticipate changes in property values and rental income potential, adjusting their strategies to either capitalize on price increases or avoid overpaying in uncertain markets.

Employment Rates and Market Stability

Employment rates play a crucial role in shaping real estate demand. High employment typically means more people have stable incomes and are therefore more likely to purchase homes, creating demand in both the rental and ownership markets. When employment is low, however, fewer people can afford to buy, which can result in a softer market, especially in areas heavily affected by layoffs or economic downturns.

Real estate leader Tom Daniels highlights this in his approach: "I always look at job growth as an indicator of market stability. If a city or region is seeing an increase in jobs, it's a good sign for real estate, as new jobs often lead to increased demand for housing, whether in rentals or sales. In cities with low employment growth, I focus on value properties or rentals, where I can wait for a more favorable economic climate."

Employment rates can be particularly useful for those investing in regions undergoing significant economic changes. Watching job trends allows investors to identify areas poised for growth and avoid markets at risk of decline.

Bringing It All Together

Each of these economic indicators—interest rates, inflation, and employment—provides a different lens through which to view and understand real estate trends. Savvy investors and professionals pay close attention to these economic signals, recognizing that they shape buyer behavior, property values, and market demand. By integrating this broader economic knowledge with market-specific insights, real estate professionals are better equipped to time their moves strategically, making choices that align with both local market conditions and the larger economic environment. This awareness enables them not just to respond to current conditions but to anticipate what lies ahead, crafting resilient and flexible investment strategies.

Identifying and Understanding Market Cycles

The real estate market, much like the economy itself, moves in cycles. These cycles—expansion, peak, contraction, and recovery—shape investment opportunities and risk, impacting how and when real estate professionals buy, sell, or hold properties. Understanding where the market is within this cycle allows investors to adapt their strategies to maximize returns and minimize risks.

The Expansion Phase: Growth and Opportunity

The expansion phase is marked by increased demand for properties, rising prices, and growing development. During this phase, economic indicators such as employment rates and GDP growth are typically strong, and buyer confidence is high. As a result, properties tend to appreciate, and new construction projects often surge as developers aim to meet demand.

During expansion, investors often take advantage of the favorable market conditions by actively acquiring properties and selling them for profit as prices rise. Residential and commercial markets alike see growth, with increased demand for housing, retail spaces, and office buildings. Real estate broker Linda Perez explains, "In an expansion phase, I focus on acquiring properties that are positioned to appreciate quickly. It's a time when buyer competition is strong, so finding good deals early and taking decisive action is crucial to securing valuable assets."

The expansion phase can be lucrative, but it also requires investors to be cautious, as the market will eventually reach its peak. Understanding when a particular region or property type has nearly maximized its growth potential is essential to avoid overpaying or investing in assets that may lose value in the next phase.

The Peak: High Prices and Increased Competition

As the market reaches its peak, demand and prices are at their highest. This phase is often characterized by fierce competition among buyers and investors, driving prices to levels that may not be sustainable. Properties sell quickly, often at inflated prices, and the supply of available properties becomes increasingly scarce. While the peak can offer profitable selling opportunities, it's also a time to exercise caution, as any investment made at the peak carries a heightened risk if the market turns.

Investors and professionals should pay close attention to economic indicators during this stage. Signs that the market may be overheating, such as an unsustainable rise in prices or increasing vacancy rates, often signal the approach of a contraction phase. During the peak, experienced investors may shift their strategies from buying to selling or holding, locking in gains before a potential downturn.

Developer Mark Fisher shares his strategy for managing the peak: "At this stage, I tend to focus on offloading properties that have already appreciated significantly, rather than trying to acquire new ones at inflated prices. Timing the peak is challenging, but if you have assets that are performing well, it can be a smart move to realize those gains before the cycle shifts."

The Contraction and Recovery Phases: Risks and Opportunities

Following the peak, the market often enters a contraction phase, where prices decline, demand wanes, and unsold inventory can build up. This phase, commonly known as a downturn or correction, is often accompanied by lower buyer confidence, rising interest rates, or economic setbacks that reduce the pool of active buyers. While contraction may seem like a time to avoid real estate investments, it can offer unique opportunities, especially for those seeking discounted properties or long-term value investments.

During contraction, properties may be priced below their intrinsic value, allowing investors to acquire them at a discount with the expectation of future appreciation. Real estate expert Nancy Lee emphasizes the importance of patience during a downturn: "I've seen many fortunes made by those who had the patience to buy when others were fearful. When the market is down, that's when I start looking for undervalued properties in high-potential areas. It requires a longer-term mindset, but the opportunities can be tremendous."

After contraction, the market eventually transitions into recovery. In this phase, economic indicators begin to stabilize, demand gradually increases, and property values start to rise again. Recovery provides opportunities for investors to get in early, acquiring assets at favorable prices before the next expansion phase. The recovery phase often presents the best balance between affordability and growth potential, making it an ideal time to invest.

Navigating Market Cycles for Long-Term Success

Understanding market cycles gives real estate professionals a powerful tool for strategic decision-making. Recognizing which phase the market is in allows them to adapt their approaches—whether by aggressively investing during expansion, capitalizing on peak selling opportunities, or patiently acquiring undervalued properties during contraction. By aligning investment strategies with market cycles, real estate investors can optimize their returns, capitalize on growth opportunities, and navigate downturns with resilience.

The ability to identify and respond to market cycles is one of the hallmarks of successful real estate professionals. Rather than fearing downturns or relying solely on booms, seasoned investors use these cycles to their advantage, creating a balanced and sustainable approach to real estate that can weather the highs and lows of the market.

Chapter 2: Building a Winning Mindset

Embracing Resilience and Adaptability
In real estate, resilience and adaptability are the cornerstones of a winning mindset. The market is a constantly shifting landscape—interest rates fluctuate, property values ebb and flow, and economic conditions can change unexpectedly. Professionals who thrive in this environment are those who can remain calm in the face of challenges and adapt their strategies as needed. Resilience and adaptability don't just help you survive difficult times; they allow you to seize opportunities that others might overlook.

The Importance of Resilience

Resilience is the ability to bounce back from setbacks and keep moving forward. In real estate, setbacks are common, whether it's a deal that falls through, a property that doesn't sell, or an unexpected market downturn. Those who are resilient don't dwell on failures; instead, they see them as learning opportunities and use them to build a stronger approach for the future.

Take the story of industry leader Emily Ortiz, a seasoned investor with a background in residential properties. Early in her career, she faced a significant challenge when a major deal she'd worked on for months fell apart at the last minute. "It was a tough blow," she recalls, "but I realized I had two choices: I could let it derail me, or I could use it as fuel to find an even better opportunity." Rather than allowing disappointment to hold her back, Emily quickly shifted her focus and went on to close one of her most profitable deals just a few months later. Her resilience not only helped her recover from a setback but also strengthened her resolve and confidence.

Resilience isn't just about moving on from disappointments—it's about maintaining a positive outlook and using each experience as a stepping stone toward success. Real estate is a long game, and those who thrive are the ones who don't give up, even when the going gets tough.

Adapting to Market Shifts

Adaptability is just as important as resilience. The real estate market is unpredictable, and conditions can shift with little warning. Successful professionals know that what worked yesterday may not work tomorrow. They're constantly learning, refining their strategies, and adapting to new realities. This adaptability allows them to stay ahead of the curve, turning potential challenges into opportunities.

For instance, during a sudden economic downturn, many real estate professionals pull back, waiting for more stable conditions. However, some of the most successful investors take a different approach—they adapt. They shift their focus to emerging opportunities, such as buying undervalued properties or exploring new markets. Veteran agent Brian Chen explains, "In times of market uncertainty, I look for the hidden gems. That adaptability has allowed me to find deals that others might miss because they're too focused on the immediate risk."

Adapting to market shifts doesn't mean abandoning a strategy at the first sign of trouble. Instead, it means being open to new ideas, re-evaluating the plan, and making adjustments as necessary. Real estate professionals who are adaptable know how to read the market and adjust their approach without losing sight of their long-term goals.

Practical Techniques for Building Resilience and Adaptability

Cultivating resilience and adaptability takes intentional effort. One way to build resilience is through reframing challenges. Instead of seeing a setback as a failure, try viewing it as feedback. Ask yourself: "What can I learn from this? How can I use this experience to make better decisions in the future?" By focusing on growth rather than dwelling on the setback, you build a mindset that's ready for any challenge.

Another practical approach is proactive problem-solving. Anticipate potential obstacles and think through possible solutions ahead of time. If you're entering a market known for high competition, consider how you might differentiate your offers. If you're dealing with fluctuating interest rates, explore creative financing options. By preparing in advance, you develop flexibility and confidence, making it easier to adjust your strategy when circumstances change.

Embracing Challenges as Opportunities

Resilience and adaptability aren't just traits—they're skills that can be cultivated through experience and practice. In real estate, challenges are inevitable, but each one is an opportunity to grow stronger, wiser, and more strategic. Embrace setbacks as a natural part of the journey and adapt as you learn, knowing that each adjustment brings you closer to mastering the complexities of the market. The professionals who excel in this field aren't those who avoid challenges but those who meet them head-on, using resilience and adaptability to turn obstacles into stepping stones toward success.

Fostering a Long-Term Vision

In real estate, one of the most valuable assets a professional can have is a long-term vision. Markets fluctuate, deals fall through, and challenges arise. However, those who maintain a clear vision and focus on the bigger picture are more likely to succeed over time. A long-term perspective enables you to navigate the ups and downs with patience and purpose, knowing that each step, each transaction, is building toward a larger goal.

Setting a Long-Term Vision

The first step in developing a long-term mindset is defining what success means to you in real estate. Are you focused on building a portfolio of rental properties, becoming an expert in commercial real estate, or creating a niche within luxury markets? Setting specific, measurable goals provides direction and purpose, helping you to make decisions that align with your ultimate objectives. Without this clarity, it's easy to get sidetracked by short-term fluctuations, which can lead to impulsive decisions and missed opportunities.

Consider the approach taken by real estate investor and developer Carla Ruiz. Early in her career, Carla set a goal to create a portfolio of multi-family rental properties that would provide steady income over the long term. "I knew that I wanted to build something sustainable," she explains. "It wasn't about quick wins; it was about building wealth that would last." With this clear vision in mind, Carla was able to stay focused, even during times when the market was volatile. Her long-term perspective kept her grounded, allowing her to prioritize investments that fit her goals rather than getting distracted by short-term trends.

Setting a long-term vision also means being realistic about the journey ahead. Real estate is a field where rewards often come after years of hard work, not overnight. By embracing a mindset that values steady, incremental progress, you'll be better prepared to handle setbacks and keep moving forward.

Creating Incremental Milestones

While a long-term vision is essential, achieving it often requires breaking it down into manageable steps. Establishing incremental milestones—such as acquiring your first property, reaching a certain level of cash flow, or building a network of reliable contacts—provides you with tangible goals to work toward along the way. These milestones serve as markers of progress, motivating you to keep pushing forward and celebrate the small victories that lead to bigger achievements.

Real estate leader David Patel illustrates this well. His goal was to develop a portfolio of sustainable properties across several states. Instead of rushing to acquire multiple properties at once, he focused on one property at a time, ensuring each was profitable before moving on to the next. "I knew that I'd get there eventually," David shares. "Each property I added was a step toward that vision, and having those smaller milestones made the journey manageable and rewarding."

Creating milestones can also help you stay adaptable. As the market changes, you may find that certain goals need to be adjusted, whether it's the timing of a purchase or the type of property you're investing in. By focusing on incremental steps, you can adapt without losing sight of your overarching vision.

The Power of Patience in Real Estate

Patience is a cornerstone of a long-term mindset, especially in a field like real estate, where market conditions can shift dramatically. During economic downturns or slow markets, it's tempting to become reactive, either by making hasty decisions to cut losses or by stepping away entirely. But real estate professionals with a long-term vision know that downturns are temporary, and they often see them as opportunities rather than obstacles.

Experienced investor Sarah Lee shares her perspective on patience: "In real estate, timing is everything, but it doesn't mean acting on impulse. During a downturn, I look at it as a time to prepare and strengthen my foundation, knowing that when the market rebounds, I'll be ready to act." Her ability to maintain a steady approach has helped her grow a successful portfolio, avoiding rash decisions that could undermine her long-term goals.

Patience also allows you to make decisions with a level head, without the pressure of immediate gains. It means taking the time to find the right property, conduct thorough due diligence, and ensure a good deal rather than settling for a quick but potentially unwise investment. This approach is often what separates successful professionals from those who burn out quickly.

Embracing the Long Game

A long-term vision helps you see the bigger picture and stay motivated, even during challenging times. Real estate is a journey, one that requires resilience, patience, and a commitment to continuous learning. By setting a clear vision, creating achievable milestones, and practicing patience, you're laying the groundwork for sustainable success. Embracing this mindset transforms real estate from a series of transactions into a fulfilling and strategic career path, where each choice is a building block toward a rewarding future.

With a long-term perspective, you'll not only weather the inevitable ups and downs but also position yourself to capitalize on opportunities that align with your vision. This is the path to lasting success in real estate—a journey built not on fleeting gains but on enduring growth and purpose.

Cultivating Confidence and Decisiveness

Confidence and decisiveness are essential qualities for success in real estate. In a field where opportunities often arise quickly and competition is fierce, the ability to make clear, confident decisions can set you apart. These traits don't always come naturally, but with experience, practice, and a focus on personal growth, you can build the confidence necessary to make bold choices and take calculated risks that propel you forward.

Building Confidence Through Knowledge and Preparation

Confidence in real estate starts with knowledge. The more you know about the market, property types, investment strategies, and legalities, the more empowered you'll feel when making decisions. Confidence isn't about always having the "right" answer; it's about trusting in your preparation and ability to respond to whatever comes your way.

Take the approach of seasoned broker and investor Max Hamilton. Early in his career, Max spent countless hours studying market trends, property analysis, and negotiation tactics. "I knew that if I wanted to make sound decisions, I had to build a foundation of knowledge," Max says. "When you're prepared, you're less likely to hesitate because you know you're making an informed choice." This thorough preparation allowed Max to make confident offers, engage in negotiations, and communicate effectively with clients, building trust and establishing himself as a reliable professional in the industry.

Preparation doesn't mean overthinking. Instead, it's about gathering the necessary information, conducting due diligence, and then trusting in your skills and instincts. When you know you've done your homework, you're less likely to second-guess yourself and more likely to act decisively, a trait highly valued in real estate.

Developing Decisiveness Through Experience and Reflection

Decisiveness is the ability to make quick, informed decisions without unnecessary hesitation. In real estate, this quality is crucial. Properties can move quickly, and missing out on a good deal because of indecision can be costly. But decisiveness is more than just making quick choices; it's about balancing speed with good judgment. Developing this skill requires experience, reflection, and learning from both successes and setbacks.

Real estate developer and mentor Carla Jensen explains her approach: "When I first started, I was overly cautious, afraid to commit without knowing every detail. But over time, I realized that hesitation was costing me opportunities. So I began trusting my instincts more and reflecting on each decision to learn from it, whether it went well or not." By reflecting on her experiences, Carla was able to improve her judgment and make more decisive choices. Today, she attributes much of her success to her ability to assess situations quickly and act confidently.

Reflection after each transaction or decision—whether it's a deal, a negotiation, or a new partnership—provides valuable insights. When you take time to evaluate what went well and what could have been improved, you refine your decision-making process. This experience-driven approach helps you become more decisive without sacrificing thoughtfulness.

Overcoming Fear of Failure

One of the biggest barriers to confidence and decisiveness in real estate is the fear of failure. Real estate deals involve high stakes, and the potential for loss can feel daunting. However, successful professionals learn to view failure not as an endpoint but as part of the learning process. Embracing the possibility of failure and seeing it as an opportunity for growth can free you from hesitation, empowering you to take calculated risks.

Investor and property manager Janet Roberts recounts her journey in overcoming the fear of failure. Early in her career, Janet missed out on several lucrative deals because she was paralyzed by "what if" questions. "Eventually, I realized that my fear of failing was holding me back more than the actual risk of failure ever could," Janet reflects. "Once I accepted that failure is sometimes part of the process, I started making bolder decisions, and that's when my career really took off."

To build confidence, it's essential to reframe your mindset around risk and failure. Remind yourself that each decision is a step forward, regardless of the outcome. Rather than dwelling on potential mistakes, focus on the lessons each experience offers. With this perspective, you'll find it easier to make confident decisions without being weighed down by fear.

Acting with Confidence and Purpose

Confidence and decisiveness don't mean never making a mistake; they mean moving forward with purpose, trusting in your skills, and committing to a course of action. In real estate, confidence inspires trust—clients, partners, and investors are more likely to work with someone who exudes certainty and direction. Decisiveness, meanwhile, allows you to act quickly when opportunities arise, ensuring you don't miss out because of doubt or hesitation.

Cultivating these qualities takes time, but they are invaluable assets for anyone serious about succeeding in real estate. By building your knowledge base, learning from your experiences, and reframing your mindset around risk, you can develop the confidence and decisiveness needed to thrive in this competitive field. When you believe in your ability to make sound choices, you unlock your potential to seize opportunities and grow your real estate career with conviction and resilience.

Chapter 3: Strategic Networking and Relationship B

Building a Professional Network in Real Estate
In real estate, success often depends on the strength and reach of your professional network. Relationships are the foundation of the industry, influencing everything from deal flow to finding trusted partners for transactions. A strong network connects you with investors, agents, contractors, lenders, and other key players who can open doors, provide guidance, and offer support through the complexities of real estate transactions. Building this network takes time and strategy, but the benefits can be transformative.

Identifying Key Players
When starting to build a network, it's essential to know who the key players are and how they fit into your specific goals. Depending on your focus—whether it's residential sales, commercial investment, property management, or development—you'll want to connect with people who are relevant to your niche. For example, residential agents and property managers may prioritize relationships with mortgage lenders, inspectors, and local contractors. On the other hand, commercial investors might fo-

cus on networking with potential investors, financial analysts, and developers.

Networking expert and veteran real estate investor Tony Vargas emphasizes the importance of intentionality in building a network. "You don't need to know everyone, but you need to know the right people," he explains. "Identify the areas where you need support or guidance and find those who can provide it. Quality over quantity is key." Being strategic in who you connect with allows you to build a network that aligns with your professional goals, saving you time and effort and yielding more impactful relationships.

Attending Industry Events and Utilizing Social Media

Industry events are one of the best avenues for networking in real estate. Conferences, seminars, workshops, and meet-ups bring together professionals across the industry, providing a perfect setting to make connections. Attending events that focus on your area of interest allows you to meet like-minded professionals, stay updated on market trends, and participate in discussions relevant to your field. Make it a goal to attend a few industry events each year, as they offer invaluable opportunities to learn and network.

Social media has also transformed the way professionals connect, making it easier to stay in touch and expand your reach. Platforms like LinkedIn allow you to connect with professionals beyond your immediate geographical area, while Instagram and Facebook groups focused on real estate provide forums to exchange ideas and share knowledge. Many top real estate professionals maintain an active presence on social media, using it not only to stay connected but also to share insights and establish their expertise.

Seasoned real estate agent Lisa Tran uses a combined approach of in-person networking and social media to build her connections. "After meeting someone at an event, I connect with them on LinkedIn and follow their updates. It keeps me on their radar, and I can reach out if there's a project we might collaborate on." This approach of blending traditional networking with digital follow-up creates a robust and sustainable network.

Maintaining and Strengthening Your Connections

Building a network is not just about making introductions; it's about nurturing those relationships over time. Real estate is a relationship-driven industry, and maintaining consistent communication is crucial. A quick check-in email, a message on social media, or inviting contacts to coffee or lunch meetings can keep relationships warm and genuine. Small gestures, like sending congratulations on a new deal or remembering a colleague's birthday, go a long way in building goodwill and keeping you top of mind.

Lender and real estate consultant Ben Carter has seen the impact of consistent relationship-building firsthand. "Early in my career, I made it a habit to reach out to my contacts every few months. Sometimes it was just to catch up or share market insights. Over time, this simple habit led to referrals, partnerships, and even lifelong friendships." By prioritizing consistent contact, Ben cultivated a network that became an invaluable resource throughout his career.

Creating a Network That Lasts

A robust professional network doesn't happen overnight, but with patience, intention, and consistent effort, you can build a circle of connections that supports your growth and success in real estate. The people you meet today might be your partners, mentors, or collaborators tomorrow. By strategically identifying key contacts, attending events, using social media, and nurturing relationships, you'll create a network that not only provides immediate opportunities but also sustains you for years to come. In real estate, as in life, relationships are investments—and with the right care, they yield exceptional returns.

Building Trust and Lasting Relationships

Trust is the foundation of every successful relationship in real estate. In an industry where large sums of money and high-stakes decisions are involved, people want to work with those they can rely on—professionals who demonstrate integrity, transparency, and a commitment to doing what's right. Building trust isn't a one-time effort; it's a process that takes consistent, ethical behavior and genuine care for others. When trust is established, relationships become more than transactional—they become long-lasting, mutually beneficial partnerships.

The Role of Integrity and Transparency

In real estate, integrity is everything. People want to know that they are working with someone who is honest, ethical, and straightforward. Practicing integrity means being transparent in all transactions, providing accurate information, and being open about any potential issues or risks. For example, if a property has drawbacks, a trustworthy professional will communicate these openly rather than hiding them for the sake of a quick sale. This level of honesty may seem challenging at first, but it creates a reputation that attracts loyal clients and colleagues who value integrity.

Real estate broker Maria Jackson shares how integrity has been central to her career. "Early on, I learned that honesty, even when it's uncomfortable, builds credibility. I've had clients come back to me years later because they trusted me to tell them the whole truth, not just the parts that would lead to a sale. They know I care about their long-term success, not just my commission." Maria's commitment to transparency has allowed her to build a strong reputation, ensuring repeat business and referrals from clients who trust her implicitly.

Trust grows when clients and colleagues know they're dealing with someone who will be truthful, even if it means short-term sacrifice. This level of transparency not only solidifies relationships but also builds a reputation that others in the industry respect.

Reliability and Follow-Through

Reliability is another cornerstone of trust. In real estate, reliability means following through on commitments, responding promptly, and being there when needed. Simple acts, such as showing up on time, delivering on promises, and communicating effectively, all contribute to a reputation for dependability. In an industry where delays or miscommunications can lead to lost deals, reliability is invaluable.

Consider the approach of property manager Mark Evans, who has built his business on consistent, reliable service. "I make it a point to keep my word, even on the small things," Mark explains. "If I say I'll get back to someone by a certain date, I do. If I promise a certain level of service, I deliver it. People know they can count on me, and that trust has led to some of my best business relationships." By consistently honoring his commitments, Mark has created a network of clients, vendors, and colleagues who value his dependability.

Reliability builds trust over time. When people see that you're dependable, they're more likely to work with you on future projects, refer you to others, and collaborate on larger endeavors.

Fostering Genuine Relationships

Building trust in real estate also requires sincerity. People can sense when interactions are purely transactional, and they respond far more positively to those who show genuine interest in their needs and goals. Taking the time to get to know clients, colleagues, and partners on a personal level goes a long way in establishing trust. Asking about their families, remembering important details about their lives, or celebrating their achievements fosters goodwill and strengthens the relationship beyond business.

Veteran investor Julia Thompson takes a genuine approach to her relationships. "For me, it's not just about the deal—it's about the people. I try to understand what's important to them, what they're working toward. When people see that I care about their success, they trust me more, and that trust often leads to lasting partnerships." Julia's ability to foster genuine relationships has been key to her longevity and success in the industry.

Trust isn't just built through business deals; it's strengthened by personal connections. Real estate is a relationship-based business, and showing an interest in the people behind the transactions creates bonds that endure beyond individual deals.

The Benefits of a Trust-Based Reputation

In real estate, a trust-based reputation is priceless. When clients and colleagues trust you, they're more likely to recommend you, partner with you, and seek your advice. This reputation becomes a self-sustaining asset, leading to a continuous flow of opportunities, referrals, and collaborations. Trust takes time to build, but it yields significant long-term rewards, creating a network that is supportive, loyal, and mutually beneficial.

By committing to integrity, reliability, and genuine relationships, you lay the foundation for a career built on trust. This approach not only enhances your professional reputation but also opens doors to partnerships and opportunities that last a lifetime. In real estate, a reputation for trustworthiness is one of the most valuable assets you can cultivate—and it will serve you well in every relationship you build.

Leveraging Relationships for Growth and Success

Building a network of trusted relationships in real estate is only the beginning. To truly benefit from these connections, you need to actively leverage them in ways that contribute to growth and mutual success. Strategic relationships can provide access to new deals, open doors to new markets, offer valuable mentorship, and enhance credibility. By fostering a network built on trust and mutual benefit, you can transform relationships into lasting partnerships that support both your own goals and those of your contacts.

The Power of Partnerships and Joint Ventures

One of the most powerful ways to leverage relationships is through partnerships and joint ventures. Real estate often requires significant capital, specialized skills, and access to specific markets or networks. By partnering with others who bring complementary strengths, you can take on larger projects, spread risks, and capitalize on shared resources. Whether it's teaming up with an investor to acquire a property, collaborating with a developer for a new project, or joining forces with a marketing expert to attract buyers, partnerships expand your capacity and reach.

Real estate investor and developer Carl Reed attributes much of his success to strategic partnerships. "Early on, I partnered with someone who had capital but didn't have the time to manage the project. I was able to bring my management skills to the table, and together, we both achieved more than we could have individually. That first partnership set the foundation for many successful ventures since," Carl explains. By pooling resources and sharing responsibilities, Carl created a mutually beneficial arrangement that accelerated his growth and built lasting professional alliances.

Partnerships are most successful when both parties bring something valuable to the table. Whether it's knowledge, capital, or connections, identify what you can offer and seek out people whose skills and resources complement your own. This way, the partnership is balanced, fostering trust and ensuring that both sides have a vested interest in the project's success.

Gaining Referrals and Recommendations

Referrals are the lifeblood of real estate, and a strong network can lead to a steady stream of new business opportunities. When clients, colleagues, and partners trust you, they are more likely to recommend you to others, whether it's a property owner seeking a reliable agent, an investor looking for a promising deal, or a buyer searching for a new home. These referrals not only bring in new clients but also lend credibility, as potential clients are more likely to trust you if they were referred by someone they know.

Top-producing real estate agent Linda Chung has built her career largely through referrals. "When clients trust you, they tell others about you," Linda shares. "I make it a priority to nurture my relationships, and over the years, I've been fortunate to have clients refer me to their friends, family, and colleagues. Those referrals are more valuable than any advertising I could pay for." Linda's focus on client satisfaction and relationship-building has created a network that consistently brings her new business without the need for constant marketing.

To encourage referrals, stay in touch with your contacts, offer value even when there's no immediate transaction, and express gratitude when referrals come your way. A simple thank-you note or a small gesture of appreciation can go a long way in reinforcing the relationship, making contacts more likely to recommend you in the future.

Providing Value and Staying Engaged

One of the most effective ways to leverage your network is by consistently providing value and staying engaged. When you contribute to your contacts' success—whether by sharing insights, connecting them with helpful resources, or offering assistance—they are more inclined to support you in return. Providing value doesn't have to be complicated; it can be as simple as sending a market update, sharing an interesting article, or offering to introduce someone to a helpful contact.

Experienced property manager Tom Rivers has made providing value a core part of his networking approach. "I try to be a resource for my network," Tom explains. "If I see an article that could benefit someone or hear about a potential investment that aligns with a contact's interests, I share it with them. It's not about expecting something in return; it's about building goodwill. But over time, those small gestures often lead to opportunities and collaborations."

Maintaining engagement with your network doesn't require constant communication but rather meaningful touchpoints that show you care about their success. Whether it's a quarterly check-in or a quick message on social media, regular engagement keeps you top of mind and positions you as a valuable connection. As you provide value, your network becomes more willing to reciprocate, offering support and opportunities when you need them.

Building a Network That Grows With You

By leveraging relationships strategically, you're not just expanding your reach—you're building a support system that grows with you throughout your career. A well-nurtured network can offer mentorship, partnerships, and new deals at every stage of your journey. Real estate is an industry where personal connections drive professional growth, and by cultivating relationships based on trust, value, and mutual benefit, you create a network that supports sustainable success.

In the end, leveraging your relationships isn't just about seeking what others can offer you; it's about creating a community where everyone benefits. Approach each relationship with a mindset of collaboration and reciprocity, and you'll build a network that not only enhances your career but enriches the careers of those around you. The connections you make today are the foundation for the opportunities of tomorrow, and with the right approach, your network will be one of the most powerful assets in your real estate journey.

Chapter 4: Mastering Negotiations

Essential Negotiation Techniques and Tactics
In the world of real estate, mastering negotiation techniques can mean the difference between securing a great deal and losing out. Effective negotiation isn't about overpowering the other party; it's about strategically using skills and techniques to achieve mutually beneficial results. By employing specific tactics, staying composed, and knowing how to respond under pressure, real estate professionals can build confidence and increase their bargaining power in any negotiation.

Anchoring and Setting the Initial Tone

One of the most powerful tactics in negotiations is the concept of anchoring. Anchoring involves setting the initial terms or price point, establishing a starting reference for further discussion. Research shows that the initial anchor often influences the entire negotiation process, impacting how the other party perceives the value of the property or the fairness of the terms. By setting an anchor, you establish a reference point that can help sway the negotiation in your favor.

Top real estate agent Darren Cole explains how he uses anchoring effectively in his negotiations. "When I'm representing a seller, I'll set a strong initial asking price that aligns with the property's value and market trends," he says. "This establishes a clear expectation. On the other hand, when I'm representing a buyer, I might anchor lower if we're negotiating a price drop, making it clear that we're looking for value. Anchoring helps set the pace and tone of the discussion."

For an anchor to be effective, it should be reasonable and supported by market data. If you anchor too high or too low without justification, it can make the other party skeptical or dismissive. A well-chosen anchor, however, not only sets the tone but also shows the other side that you are informed and prepared.

Countering Offers and Using Silence

Countering is another essential negotiation tactic, allowing you to respond constructively to the other party's terms while keeping the conversation open. When faced with an initial offer, countering demonstrates that you're actively engaged in the negotiation and willing to explore different terms. A counteroffer can include a modified price, additional contingencies, or alternative terms that align better with your goals. By countering effectively, you maintain control of the negotiation and signal that you won't settle for terms that don't meet your expectations.

In addition to countering, silence is a powerful tool that's often underestimated in negotiations. When presented with an offer or counteroffer, many professionals feel the need to respond immediately. However, taking a moment of silence can create a sense of anticipation and pressure on the other party, often prompting them to improve their offer or adjust their terms.

Commercial real estate broker Angela Swift shares her approach: "When I receive an offer, I intentionally pause before responding. It gives me time to think, and it also puts the ball back in their court. The silence can be uncomfortable for the other side, sometimes leading them to add value to their offer or provide additional concessions to fill the gap."

Using silence allows you to evaluate the offer thoughtfully and often encourages the other party to reconsider their position. It can be a strategic move that keeps you in control without saying a word.

Managing Emotions and Staying Calm Under Pressure

Negotiations can be high-stress situations, especially when stakes are high, or emotions run strong. Staying calm and composed is essential, as showing frustration, impatience, or excitement can reveal more than you intend, weakening your position. Master negotiators maintain a calm demeanor, even if they disagree with the other party's terms or feel pressure to close a deal. Emotional control demonstrates professionalism and can prevent the other party from leveraging your reactions.

Real estate investor Tom Hargrove explains the importance of composure: "In one of my early deals, I let frustration show when the seller wouldn't budge on price, and it weakened my position. I learned that staying calm, even when things aren't going as planned, gives you the upper hand. If you keep a level head, you have the clarity to make smarter choices and maintain a stronger presence in the room."

Practicing emotional control also involves managing reactions to surprises or unexpected terms. Rather than reacting instantly, take a moment to process new information and consider how it fits into your overall strategy. A calm, measured response can turn a potential setback into an opportunity to explore alternative solutions.

Creating a Toolkit of Negotiation Skills

Anchoring, countering offers, using silence, and managing emotions are just a few of the techniques that make up a strong negotiation toolkit. By combining these tactics with your knowledge of the market and an understanding of the other party's motivations, you can approach negotiations with confidence. Every deal is unique, and the ability to adapt your approach based on the specific situation is key to mastering the art of negotiation.

In real estate, negotiation isn't about one side winning and the other losing. It's about finding a solution that both parties can feel good about. By employing these techniques thoughtfully and skillfully, you can enhance your ability to secure favorable terms, creating outcomes that work for everyone involved. When you come prepared with a solid negotiation toolkit, you'll be ready to face any challenge with confidence, no matter the complexities of the deal.

Closing the Deal with Confidence

The final stages of a negotiation are often the most critical. After hours, days, or even weeks of back-and-forth, this is the moment where all the elements come together to reach a mutually satisfying agreement. Closing the deal requires more than just a firm handshake; it involves overcoming last-minute objections, securing clear terms, and ensuring that both parties feel confident in the outcome. By mastering the art of closing, you can create a positive experience that lays the groundwork for future relationships and referrals.

Overcoming Last-Minute Objections

As you approach the final stages of a negotiation, it's not uncommon for last-minute concerns or objections to arise. These can come from either side and may include issues like unexpected costs, timing concerns, or terms that one party feels uncertain about. Instead of viewing these objections as barriers, see them as opportunities to further solidify the deal by addressing any lingering doubts.

Real estate agent and negotiator Karen Blake explains her approach to handling objections: "I see objections as a way to gain even more trust from my clients and counterparts. If a seller suddenly hesitates over the timeline, for instance, I reassure them by exploring options, like extending the closing date or arranging for a rent-back agreement. Finding creative solutions shows both sides that I'm committed to making the deal work for everyone involved."

When an objection arises, resist the urge to respond defensively. Instead, listen carefully, acknowledge the concern, and explore ways to address it. Sometimes, a small concession or adjustment can be enough to put the other party at ease, moving the negotiation toward a successful close. By addressing objections professionally and empathetically, you reinforce trust and show a genuine commitment to meeting both parties' needs.

Finalizing Terms Clearly and Thoroughly

Once objections are resolved, the next step is to confirm that all terms are clearly defined and agreed upon. Ambiguity at the closing stage can lead to misunderstandings, delays, or even the collapse of a deal. To avoid this, go through each agreed-upon term with both parties to ensure there is no confusion. This includes clarifying details like payment schedules, contingencies, repair requests, and any additional conditions that have been negotiated.

Real estate attorney Michael Chen advises that clarity is crucial at this stage: "I've seen deals unravel because one party misunderstood a minor clause. Taking the time to review every term and ensuring both sides are on the same page is vital for a smooth closing. It also builds confidence that everyone's interests are being protected."

A thorough final review not only reduces the risk of last-minute issues but also demonstrates professionalism and respect for both parties. By ensuring transparency in the terms, you create a foundation of trust that can make future interactions more seamless and mutually satisfying.

Creating a Positive Closing Experience

Closing a deal isn't just about finalizing terms; it's about creating a positive experience that leaves both parties feeling good about the outcome. This positive impression can have long-lasting benefits, including referrals, repeat business, and a reputation for professionalism. Make an effort to celebrate the agreement, whether by expressing gratitude, offering a closing gift, or simply acknowledging the effort both sides put into reaching a successful resolution.

Top broker Elena Moreno shares her approach to closing with positivity: "I always make sure my clients feel valued and appreciated. Once we've closed, I'll send a personal note thanking them for their trust and partnership. For buyers, I might include a small gift related to their new home. It's a way of leaving them with a warm impression of the process, and it reinforces that we're in this business to build relationships, not just make deals."

Going the extra mile at closing reinforces the relationship and shows that you genuinely care about the people involved. It helps turn a transactional process into a relational one, reminding clients and colleagues that they're valued. This personal touch can set you apart in a competitive market, strengthening your reputation as a professional who goes above and beyond.

Closing With Confidence and Integrity

A confident and thorough close leaves a lasting impression on everyone involved. It signals that you are not only committed to securing the best possible terms but are also invested in a positive experience for all parties. This approach helps ensure that each transaction ends on a high note, fostering goodwill and enhancing your reputation within the real estate community.

In real estate, every negotiation is an opportunity to build connections and establish yourself as a reliable, trustworthy professional. By handling the closing process with care—overcoming objections, clarifying terms, and creating a positive experience—you lay the groundwork for future partnerships, referrals, and successful deals. Each time you close a deal with confidence and integrity, you reinforce the trust others have in you, paving the way for a thriving, rewarding career in real estate.

Chapter 5

Chapter 5: Real Estate Investment Fundamentals

Evaluating Property Types and Investment Strategies

Real estate offers a range of property types and investment strategies, each with unique characteristics, benefits, and challenges. Understanding these options is essential for choosing investments that align with your financial goals, risk tolerance, and market conditions. Whether you're interested in residential properties, commercial spaces, industrial facilities, or mixed-use developments, evaluating the pros and cons of each property type can help you develop a successful investment strategy.

Residential Properties

Residential properties—such as single-family homes, multi-family units, and apartments—are popular among investors due to their steady demand and potential for consistent cash flow. With people always needing places to live, residential properties tend to be more resilient in economic downturns than some other types of real estate. Additionally, they often attract first-time investors due to lower entry costs and straightforward management requirements.

However, residential properties have their own challenges. For instance, single-family rentals rely on one tenant, so any vacancy results in a total loss of rental income. Multi-family units can help spread this risk across multiple tenants, but they often require more intensive management and maintenance. Real estate investor Sarah Patel explains, "I started with single-family homes, and as I grew more comfortable, I expanded to multi-family units to diversify my risk. Residential properties offer stability, but scaling up requires careful planning and consideration of management needs."

Commercial Properties

Commercial real estate—comprising office buildings, retail spaces, and shopping centers—provides investors with the potential for high returns and long-term leases, often with business tenants. Because businesses are generally willing to pay a premium for prime locations, commercial properties can yield higher income compared to residential rentals. Commercial leases also tend to be longer, providing more predictable income streams and reducing the frequency of turnover.

However, commercial properties can be vulnerable to economic shifts. For instance, retail spaces may struggle during economic downturns as consumer spending decreases. Additionally, commercial properties generally require more significant initial investment and may involve complex lease agreements and regulatory requirements. Real estate broker Tom Hernandez shares his experience: "Commercial real estate has been lucrative for me, but it's essential to know your tenants' business models. Understanding their stability and industry trends is key to minimizing risk."

Industrial Properties

Industrial properties—such as warehouses, distribution centers, and manufacturing facilities—are less common but offer unique investment opportunities. With the rise of e-commerce, demand for warehousing and distribution spaces has grown significantly, making industrial properties an attractive option. These properties often require less maintenance than residential or commercial buildings, and industrial leases are typically long-term, resulting in stable income.

On the downside, industrial properties are highly specialized and location-dependent. Investors need to carefully assess the industry trends and local demand, as industrial tenants may require specific logistical features, such as proximity to highways or major distribution hubs. Additionally, industrial properties can be affected by economic shifts, especially those tied to manufacturing or import/export industries.

Mixed-Use Developments

Mixed-use properties combine residential, commercial, and sometimes industrial spaces within a single development. These properties are becoming increasingly popular in urban areas where people seek convenient, multi-functional spaces. Mixed-use developments offer investors diversified revenue streams, as they cater to multiple types of tenants, and can be more resilient during economic fluctuations.

However, mixed-use developments often involve higher costs and more complex zoning and regulatory considerations. They require a broader understanding of different types of property management and may involve coordinating with multiple tenants with varying needs. Real estate developer Jamie Lin shares, "Mixed-use properties can be a fantastic investment, but they require a versatile skill set and a good understanding of local zoning laws. It's all about balance—knowing when and how to adjust the property's usage to maximize revenue."

Choosing the Right Strategy

Once you understand the different property types, the next step is to determine your investment strategy. Some investors focus on income generation through rental properties, while others look for properties with high potential for appreciation. Flipping properties, where investors buy, renovate, and sell for a profit, can yield quick returns but also comes with higher risks and requires market timing skills.

Choosing a strategy depends on your goals and resources. If you're looking for steady income with lower risk, long-term rentals in stable markets might be ideal. If you're more risk-tolerant and looking for higher returns, commercial or industrial properties might be more suitable. Experienced investor David Monroe advises, "It's essential to match your strategy with your financial goals and risk tolerance. Real estate is a diverse field, and not every property type will fit every strategy."

Finding Your Niche

Selecting the right property type and investment strategy is about finding a niche that aligns with your strengths, goals, and risk tolerance. Whether you choose residential properties for their stability, commercial spaces for their income potential, or industrial properties for their growth prospects, understanding the pros and cons of each type allows you to make informed, strategic choices. As you refine your approach, you'll develop a clearer sense of where your interests and expertise lie, setting the foundation for a successful real estate investment journey.

Understanding Cash Flow and ROI

In real estate investing, cash flow and return on investment (ROI) are two fundamental metrics that can determine the success or failure of an investment. Cash flow reflects the income generated by a property after expenses, while ROI measures the profitability of an investment relative to its cost. Together, these metrics provide a clear picture of a property's financial health and its potential to meet your financial goals. By understanding how to calculate and interpret cash flow and ROI, you can make more informed investment decisions that align with your objectives.

Calculating Cash Flow

Cash flow is the net income you receive from a property after deducting all expenses. Positive cash flow means the property is generating more income than it costs to maintain, while negative cash flow indicates that expenses are exceeding income. For real estate investors, positive cash flow is often a key objective, as it provides steady income and enhances the property's overall profitability.

To calculate cash flow, start by determining your monthly rental income. Then subtract the monthly expenses associated with the property, which may include mortgage payments, property taxes, insurance, maintenance, property management fees, and any other operational costs. The formula is as follows:

Cash Flow = Total Rental Income - Total Expenses

For example, if you own a rental property that generates $2,000 in monthly rental income and has monthly expenses totaling $1,500, your cash flow would be $500. This positive cash flow indicates that the property is generating income beyond its costs, contributing to your financial goals.

Real estate investor Jennifer Leary emphasizes the importance of cash flow for building wealth. "I always prioritize properties with strong cash flow, even if the appreciation potential is lower. Cash flow provides a cushion against market fluctuations and helps me reinvest in additional properties," she explains. Properties with positive cash flow are generally more resilient during market downturns, as they continue generating income regardless of property value changes.

Evaluating ROI

While cash flow shows the monthly income from a property, ROI provides a broader view of an investment's profitability over time. ROI measures how much profit you're earning relative to the amount you invested in the property. A higher ROI indicates a more profitable investment, but it's essential to consider factors like market trends, location, and property type, as these can impact the long-term value of your investment.

The basic formula for ROI is:

ROI = (Net Profit / Total Investment Cost) x 100

Net profit is the income earned from the property after expenses, including the cash flow over a set period (usually a year), and any appreciation in property value. The total investment cost includes the purchase price, closing costs, renovation expenses, and any other capital outlay required to make the property income-generating.

For example, if you purchased a property for $150,000, invested $20,000 in renovations, and made $10,000 in net profit after one year, your total investment cost is $170,000. The ROI would be:

ROI = ($10,000 / $170,000) x 100 = 5.88%

This 5.88% ROI helps you compare the profitability of this property to other investments, allowing you to prioritize properties with higher returns.

Setting Cash Flow and ROI Targets

Establishing clear cash flow and ROI targets is essential for achieving your financial goals. Many investors set minimum thresholds for cash flow and ROI based on their income needs, risk tolerance, and investment strategy. For example, an investor focused on generating passive income might prioritize properties with a higher cash flow, while someone interested in long-term wealth building may target a higher ROI through appreciation potential.

Real estate consultant Michael Tran suggests setting realistic targets that align with market conditions. "When I evaluate properties, I aim for a cash flow that provides at least a 6% yield and an ROI of 8-10% annually. This ensures that I'm building wealth steadily without overextending my risk," he explains. By setting specific targets, you create a benchmark for assessing properties, making it easier to filter out investments that don't align with your objectives.

Interpreting Cash Flow and ROI in Context

Cash flow and ROI should not be evaluated in isolation; they are part of a larger financial picture. Properties with high cash flow may have lower appreciation potential, while properties with strong ROI might yield lower immediate cash flow. The location, property type, and current market conditions all impact these metrics, and understanding their context can help you make more balanced decisions.

For instance, a property in a high-demand urban area might have a lower initial cash flow due to high purchase costs, but it could yield a higher ROI over time due to appreciation. Conversely, a suburban rental might provide immediate positive cash flow but have limited appreciation potential. Successful investors evaluate cash flow and ROI within the context of their overall investment strategy, balancing immediate income needs with long-term growth.

Making Informed Investment Decisions

By mastering cash flow and ROI, you empower yourself to make informed, data-driven decisions. These metrics provide insight into a property's profitability and help you identify investments that align with your goals, whether you're seeking steady cash flow, high returns, or a combination of both. With a clear understanding of these fundamentals, you'll be better equipped to evaluate potential properties, optimize your portfolio, and build a solid foundation for financial success in real estate investing.

Financing Options for Real Estate Investments

Financing is a critical component of real estate investing, as the type of financing you choose can significantly impact your cash flow, returns, and risk. With multiple options available, understanding the pros and cons of each financing method helps you make informed decisions that align with your investment strategy and financial goals. From traditional mortgages to creative funding solutions, choosing the right financing option enables you to maximize your purchasing power while managing costs effectively.

Traditional Mortgages

Traditional mortgages are one of the most common ways to finance real estate purchases. Typically provided by banks or mortgage lenders, these loans offer fixed or variable interest rates and repayment terms ranging from 15 to 30 years. Traditional mortgages are especially popular for residential properties, as they often have competitive interest rates and are straightforward to obtain for qualified borrowers with stable income and good credit.

For investors looking to build a portfolio of rental properties, traditional mortgages offer a stable, predictable payment structure, making it easier to plan for cash flow. However, it's essential to consider down payment requirements, which can range from 15-25% for investment properties. Additionally, most lenders set a cap on the number of mortgages an individual can hold, which could limit your ability to expand your portfolio solely through traditional loans.

Experienced investor Caroline Flores has used traditional mortgages to finance her single-family rental properties. "A traditional mortgage offers stability, which is ideal for rental income properties," she explains. "The fixed rate gives me consistent payments, allowing me to manage cash flow effectively. It's an excellent option for long-term investors looking for steady growth without significant risk."

Private Lending and Hard Money Loans

For investors who need quick access to capital or have difficulty qualifying for traditional financing, private lending and hard money loans provide alternative solutions. Private lenders are often individuals or investment firms willing to lend money based on the property's potential rather than the borrower's credit history. Hard money lenders, on the other hand, are typically companies that specialize in short-term, high-interest loans secured by real estate assets.

These types of loans are popular among house flippers and investors involved in short-term projects, as they offer fast approval and flexibility. Hard money loans can be particularly useful for purchasing properties that require significant renovations, as traditional lenders may be hesitant to finance such projects. However, private and hard money loans come with higher interest rates, often ranging from 8-15%, and shorter repayment terms, typically between 6 months and 3 years.

Investor John Michaels has successfully used hard money loans to finance several fix-and-flip projects. "Hard money loans give me the speed and flexibility I need to acquire and renovate properties quickly," he says. "But they're not for everyone. The higher interest rate means you need a solid exit strategy, so I make sure to only use hard money for projects with quick turnaround and strong profit potential."

Real Estate Partnerships

Partnerships can be a powerful way to finance real estate investments, especially for those looking to enter larger projects without taking on excessive debt. In a partnership, two or more investors pool their resources to fund a property purchase, often bringing different strengths to the table, such as capital, expertise, or management skills. Partnerships are particularly common in commercial real estate and large-scale developments, where the capital requirements are beyond the reach of a single investor.

One of the advantages of partnerships is that they allow investors to take on larger projects and share both the risks and rewards. For example, one partner might provide the majority of the capital, while the other contributes experience in property management or construction. However, partnerships also require careful structuring and legal agreements to ensure that each party's roles, responsibilities, and profit shares are clearly defined.

Real estate developer Sarah Kim has successfully leveraged partnerships in her commercial projects. "Working with partners has allowed me to expand into markets and property types that I wouldn't have been able to tackle alone," Sarah explains. "We each bring something different to the table, and that diversity strengthens the investment. Just be sure to structure the agreement carefully, as good partnerships rely on clear communication and mutual respect."

Creative Financing Solutions

In addition to traditional and alternative loans, there are several creative financing options that investors can use to acquire properties, often with minimal upfront cash. Options like seller financing, lease options, and subject-to financing allow investors to structure deals in ways that benefit both the buyer and seller. For instance, in seller financing, the seller acts as the lender, allowing the buyer to make payments directly to them rather than obtaining a bank loan. This can be advantageous when traditional financing isn't feasible or when the seller is motivated to sell quickly.

Lease options, also known as rent-to-own, allow investors to lease a property with the option to purchase it later, providing a period to evaluate the property's income potential before committing to ownership. Subject-to financing allows an investor to take over a seller's existing mortgage without formally assuming it, offering a lower-cost entry into property ownership.

Creative financing can be highly beneficial for investors with limited capital or those seeking flexibility in financing terms.

However, these methods can be complex and often require legal guidance to structure correctly. Real estate consultant Mark Taylor advises investors to approach creative financing with caution. "Creative financing can open doors that traditional loans can't, but it requires a good understanding of the legal and financial aspects involved. When done right, though, it's a powerful tool for building a portfolio without over-leveraging."

Choosing the Right Financing Option

Selecting the right financing option depends on your investment strategy, financial situation, and the property type. Traditional mortgages are ideal for stable, long-term investments, while private loans and partnerships offer flexibility for short-term or high-capital projects. Creative financing provides unique opportunities for those willing to navigate alternative structures. By understanding the advantages and limitations of each financing method, you can tailor your approach to your investment goals, ensuring you have the financial backing to grow and succeed in real estate.

Ultimately, financing is a strategic decision that impacts every aspect of your investment. With the right funding approach, you can maximize your purchasing power, reduce risks, and create a foundation for sustainable growth in real estate.

Chapter 6:
Financing and Leveraging Capital

Exploring Financing Options and Their Benefits
In real estate investing, financing is a powerful tool that can help you acquire properties, grow your portfolio, and achieve financial goals more quickly. But with a wide range of financing options available, from traditional mortgages to alternative loans, choosing the right one is crucial. Each option has its benefits, limitations, and suitability depending on the type of investment, your financial situation, and long-term objectives. Understanding these options will help you secure the most favorable financing for your unique needs.

Traditional Mortgages

Traditional mortgages, provided by banks and lending institutions, are one of the most common forms of real estate financing. These loans offer fixed or variable interest rates over extended repayment terms, usually 15 to 30 years. For many investors, traditional mortgages are attractive because they offer lower interest rates compared to other financing options, making monthly payments more manageable and predictable.

Traditional mortgages are ideal for investors interested in long-term rental properties or primary residences. They are generally easier to qualify for if you have a strong credit history, stable income, and a sizable down payment, typically around 20% for investment properties. However, lenders often place limits on the number of mortgages an individual can hold, which can restrict the expansion of your portfolio if you rely solely on this option.

Investor Laura Evans shares her experience with traditional mortgages: "For my first few properties, I used traditional mortgages because they offered me stability. The lower interest rates made it easier to achieve positive cash flow, and the predictability of fixed payments helped me plan long-term. However, as my portfolio grew, I needed to explore other financing options to keep expanding." Traditional mortgages provide a solid foundation, but for those looking to scale their investments, they may need to be supplemented with additional financing methods.

Portfolio and Commercial Loans

For investors looking to scale their holdings, portfolio and commercial loans are popular options. Portfolio loans are held by a single lender rather than being sold on the secondary mortgage market. This means that portfolio lenders can be more flexible with their underwriting criteria, making it easier for investors to secure multiple properties within a single loan. Portfolio loans are especially useful for investors with complex financial backgrounds or those looking to finance several properties at once.

Commercial loans, on the other hand, are designed specifically for properties intended for business use, such as retail centers, apartment buildings, and office spaces. These loans often have shorter terms, typically 5-10 years, with a balloon payment due at the end. Commercial loans require higher down payments and interest rates but offer the advantage of enabling larger-scale investments and accommodating more complex business structures.

Experienced developer Mark Johnson explains his preference for portfolio loans: "When I began acquiring multiple rental properties, portfolio loans allowed me to bypass the mortgage cap imposed by traditional lenders. This flexibility gave me the freedom to grow my portfolio without the red tape, although the interest rates were slightly higher. For serious investors, portfolio loans are an effective way to scale up without getting bogged down in limitations."

Alternative Financing: Private Money and Hard Money Loans

For investors seeking quick access to capital or those who don't qualify for traditional or commercial loans, private money and hard money loans offer viable alternatives. Private money loans are sourced from individual investors or small firms who lend based on the property's potential rather than the borrower's creditworthiness. These loans often have flexible terms and can be customized to fit the borrower's needs, making them a popular choice for real estate investors involved in flipping properties or short-term projects.

Hard money loans are similar in that they are asset-based and have shorter terms, typically ranging from 6 months to 3 years. They are usually offered by private lending companies and come with higher interest rates, sometimes between 8-15%, due to the increased risk for lenders. Hard money loans are particularly beneficial for investors needing funds quickly or financing distressed properties that may not meet the strict criteria of traditional lenders.

Real estate investor Tom Riley shares his experience with hard money loans: "For my fix-and-flip projects, hard money loans have been invaluable. They give me the speed and flexibility I need to acquire properties and complete renovations. Yes, the interest is higher, but for a short-term project, it's worth it to get the deal done quickly. The key is having a clear exit strategy to avoid being overwhelmed by the high payments."

Choosing the Right Financing Option for Your Goals

Selecting the right financing option depends on your investment strategy, financial stability, and the property type. Traditional mortgages offer stability and lower rates for long-term investors, while portfolio and commercial loans provide flexibility for scaling. For those focusing on short-term projects or rapid acquisitions, private and hard money loans can be effective solutions, as long as the higher costs are carefully managed.

Each financing option has its place, and many investors find that a combination of these methods works best as their portfolios grow. By exploring and understanding the benefits and drawbacks of each financing type, you'll be well-prepared to secure the right funding, optimize cash flow, and manage growth efficiently. Ultimately, financing is about more than just securing money—it's about finding the strategic leverage that aligns with your goals and accelerates your success in real estate.

Leveraging Capital for Growth

Leveraging capital effectively can accelerate your growth as a real estate investor, enabling you to acquire more properties, increase your returns, and build a diversified portfolio. By using financing options and reinvesting equity, you can maximize your purchasing power while managing your resources responsibly. However, leveraging requires a strategic approach to balance the benefits of expanded capital with the risks of increased debt. With a clear plan, you can make the most of leverage to achieve sustainable growth in real estate.

Refinancing for Capital Access

Refinancing is one of the most effective ways to access additional capital without selling off properties. By refinancing, you replace your existing mortgage with a new loan, often at a lower interest rate or higher loan amount. Cash-out refinancing, in particular, allows you to tap into the increased equity of a property by borrowing more than what you owe. This excess cash can then be reinvested into new properties, allowing you to grow your portfolio while continuing to hold the original asset.

For example, investor Rachel King used cash-out refinancing to expand her rental property holdings. "When my first property appreciated in value, I refinanced to take advantage of the increased equity," Rachel explains. "With that cash, I was able to make a down payment on another property without depleting my savings. It was a way to leverage my initial investment to generate even more income." Refinancing can be a powerful tool for investors who want to reinvest without liquidating assets, preserving the benefits of long-term appreciation.

However, refinancing comes with costs, including closing fees and potential prepayment penalties, so it's essential to weigh these expenses against the potential returns. Additionally, refinancing increases your monthly debt obligations, so it's crucial to ensure that your cash flow can comfortably cover the new payments.

Using Home Equity Lines of Credit (HELOCs)

A Home Equity Line of Credit (HELOC) is another valuable tool for accessing capital. Unlike a refinance, a HELOC is a revolving line of credit based on the equity in your property. You can draw from the HELOC as needed, repay it, and then draw again, similar to a credit card. This flexibility makes HELOCs particularly useful for investors looking to fund renovations, repairs, or down payments on additional properties.

For instance, investor Jim Patterson used a HELOC on his primary residence to fund improvements on a rental property he owned. "A HELOC gave me the flexibility to cover renovation costs and boost the rental income of my property without committing to a large lump-sum loan," he explains. "Once the renovations were complete and the rental income increased, I was able to pay down the HELOC balance quickly, freeing it up for future projects."

HELOCs offer interest rates lower than traditional credit cards, but they can vary, especially if tied to market rates. It's essential to use HELOCs with a clear repayment strategy, as relying on them without a solid plan can lead to excessive debt. A HELOC is most effective when used for short-term needs with a clear path for repayment.

Partnerships for Shared Capital and Expertise

Another way to leverage capital without overextending your resources is by partnering with other investors. Real estate partnerships allow you to pool funds with one or more partners, giving you access to more substantial capital than you could secure individually. Partnerships are particularly beneficial for larger projects, such as commercial properties or multi-family units, where the cost and management requirements may be beyond the scope of a single investor.

In a partnership, each party typically brings something to the table—capital, experience, or connections. For example, one partner might have significant financial resources but lack real estate expertise, while another brings management experience but has limited capital. By pooling their resources, they can take on larger projects, share the risks, and benefit from each other's strengths.

Real estate developer Karen Lee describes her successful partnership approach: "My first commercial property purchase was a partnership. My partner had the capital, and I had the experience. Together, we were able to tackle a project that neither of us could have managed alone. Partnerships have allowed me to scale faster and learn from others' experiences." Partnerships allow you to access opportunities that would be otherwise out of reach and can accelerate growth while sharing both the workload and the rewards.

However, partnerships require clear communication and a solid legal structure. Each partner's responsibilities, investment amounts, and profit shares should be outlined in a partnership agreement to avoid misunderstandings and ensure a fair distribution of benefits.

Balancing Leverage and Financial Stability

While leverage can be a powerful growth tool, it's essential to maintain a balanced approach. Over-leveraging—borrowing too much relative to your income or asset base—can expose you to high financial risk, particularly in market downturns. Responsible leverage involves borrowing within your means, ensuring that each property can cover its expenses, and setting aside reserves to manage unexpected costs.

Savvy investors like Eric Johnson set clear limits on their leverage ratios. "I aim to keep my debt-to-equity ratio in check," he explains. "I don't want to be stretched so thin that a vacancy or repair cost could jeopardize my entire portfolio. By keeping my leverage at a manageable level, I can grow sustainably." Maintaining a healthy balance between debt and income protects your investments and enables you to weather market fluctuations without undue stress.

Leveraging capital effectively allows you to expand your reach in real estate without compromising financial stability. By using refinancing, HELOCs, and partnerships wisely, you can access additional capital, pursue larger projects, and accelerate your portfolio's growth. With a balanced approach, leverage can become a powerful ally in building long-term wealth in real estate.

Managing Debt and Financial Risk

While leverage can amplify growth, it also brings added debt and financial risk. Managing this risk is essential to maintaining a healthy, resilient portfolio that can withstand market fluctuations. Responsible debt management, sound cash flow practices, and contingency planning allow investors to maximize the benefits of leverage without jeopardizing financial stability. By setting boundaries, regularly reviewing finances, and preparing for unexpected downturns, you can confidently leverage capital while safeguarding your investments.

Setting Debt Thresholds and Monitoring Debt Ratios

One of the most effective ways to manage financial risk is by setting clear debt thresholds. This means determining a comfortable debt-to-income (DTI) or debt-to-equity ratio that reflects your ability to handle debt relative to your income and assets. By setting limits, you prevent over-leverage and ensure that each investment is manageable within your overall financial picture.

Experienced investor Sam Rogers keeps a close eye on his debt ratios to maintain stability across his portfolio. "I set a maximum debt threshold for myself," he shares. "If a new investment would push my debt-to-equity ratio too high, I either wait or look for alternative financing options that won't stretch me too thin. Setting limits on debt has kept me from overextending, even when market conditions are favorable."

Monitoring debt ratios helps you assess how much additional leverage your portfolio can handle, preventing the stress of high monthly payments and improving your ability to manage cash flow. For most investors, maintaining a conservative debt-to-equity ratio can provide a buffer against market changes, ensuring that each property contributes positively to the portfolio's overall health.

Maintaining Strong Cash Flow

Cash flow management is critical in leveraged real estate investments. When you borrow capital, you add monthly debt obligations that can impact profitability. Ensuring that each property generates positive cash flow, even after loan payments, helps cover operational expenses, debt payments, and other liabilities without dipping into personal funds.

Property manager and investor Rachel Kim emphasizes the importance of cash flow in risk management. "I always assess cash flow projections before making a purchase," she explains. "If a property can't cover its expenses comfortably, I reconsider the investment or negotiate for better terms. Positive cash flow isn't just about profit; it's my safety net, covering costs and keeping debt from becoming a burden." Ensuring positive cash flow creates stability, enabling you to meet debt obligations even during vacancies or unexpected expenses.

In addition to keeping cash flow positive, it's wise to maintain a cash reserve. Many investors set aside a portion of monthly rental income for an emergency fund. This reserve provides a buffer for unexpected repairs, vacancies, or other expenses, giving you more flexibility and peace of mind. By consistently reinvesting a portion of profits into reserves, you can handle disruptions without compromising your portfolio's stability.

Planning for Market Downturns and Contingencies

Market cycles are a reality in real estate, and downturns can pose significant challenges for leveraged investments. Preparing for potential market shifts through contingency planning is essential to protecting your portfolio. By having backup strategies, you can mitigate losses and maintain stability, even during challenging economic periods.

Real estate consultant Daniel Lopez takes a proactive approach to contingency planning. "I always have an exit strategy," he says. "Whether it's refinancing, holding longer, or adjusting rents, I ensure that each investment has flexibility. During a downturn, having a plan allows me to adapt instead of making hasty decisions under pressure." Having contingency options provides you with a range of responses, allowing you to navigate downturns strategically rather than reactively.

Diversifying your investments can also reduce risk. By spreading assets across different property types or locations, you minimize the impact of a localized market dip. For example, if you hold both residential rentals and commercial properties, a downturn in one sector may be offset by stable performance in the other. Diversification enhances portfolio resilience, giving you the flexibility to weather fluctuations without significant financial strain.

Balancing Opportunity with Caution

Managing debt and financial risk isn't about avoiding leverage; it's about using it responsibly. Leverage can be a powerful tool for growth, but it must be balanced with cautious financial management. This means regularly reviewing finances, adapting as markets change, and ensuring that each investment aligns with your risk tolerance and cash flow goals.

Real estate investor Grace Harper takes a balanced approach. "I use leverage to grow, but I never lose sight of cash flow and debt ratios. Each investment is carefully considered with these factors in mind," she explains. "By setting boundaries and sticking to them, I can take advantage of opportunities without risking the stability I've worked hard to build." This approach has allowed her to expand her portfolio steadily, leveraging capital while maintaining a financially sound foundation.

In real estate, managing debt and financial risk enables you to harness the benefits of leverage while minimizing potential downsides. By setting debt thresholds, ensuring positive cash flow, and planning for contingencies, you create a resilient portfolio that can adapt to market conditions. With responsible debt management, you gain the freedom to grow and invest confidently, knowing your investments are supported by a strong financial foundation.

Chapter 7: Risk Management and Due Diligence

Conducting Thorough Property Inspections and Market Analysis

In real estate investing, thorough property inspections and market analysis are foundational elements of due diligence. These steps provide crucial insights into a property's condition, potential risks, and value within its specific market, enabling investors to make informed decisions. Skipping or rushing through these steps can lead to costly mistakes, from unexpected repair expenses to overpaying for properties that don't align with market trends. Conducting a comprehensive analysis of both the property itself and the surrounding market ensures you enter each investment with eyes wide open.

Property Inspections: Identifying Physical Risks

A property inspection is an essential step in assessing a property's physical state, uncovering issues that may impact its value, safety, or functionality. Hiring a licensed inspector to examine the property's key systems—such as the foundation, electrical wiring, plumbing, roofing, and HVAC—can reveal hidden problems that might not be immediately visible. Inspections are particularly important for older properties, as they may have structural issues or outdated systems requiring costly repairs or replacements.

Real estate investor Mike Turner emphasizes the importance of inspections. "An inspection is my first line of defense. I won't close on a property until I have a detailed report on its condition. In one deal, the inspector found water damage that would have led to mold issues. Catching it early saved me thousands in potential repairs." A thorough inspection allows you to address issues in advance, negotiate repair costs, or even walk away from a deal if the property's condition doesn't align with your investment goals.

In addition to a general inspection, some investors opt for specialized assessments, such as pest inspections, environmental assessments, or radon testing, depending on the property's location and history. Each additional assessment provides a deeper understanding of potential risks, giving you the data needed to make a well-informed decision.

Market Analysis: Evaluating Neighborhood and Market Conditions

Alongside property inspections, understanding the property's surrounding market is vital to assessing its potential value and profitability. A comprehensive market analysis includes reviewing neighborhood demographics, nearby amenities, school quality, crime rates, and accessibility to transportation and employment hubs. This information helps investors determine whether the property is in a desirable area, which can impact tenant demand, property appreciation, and rental income potential.

For instance, real estate analyst Laura Rivera advises investors to examine neighborhood trends and comparable properties. "Before purchasing, I look at recent sales data, average rental prices, and neighborhood growth indicators. You want to see evidence of upward trends, like rising property values and increased demand. A market on the upswing often means better returns." This analysis provides insights into whether the property's value is likely to appreciate over time or if it's located in an area prone to stagnation or decline.

Tools like real estate websites, local market reports, and public records are invaluable for collecting data on neighborhood dynamics and property values. Additionally, visiting the area in person allows you to assess the neighborhood's character, gauge traffic patterns, and get a feel for the community, helping you make a more informed decision about the property's potential.

Creating a Due Diligence Checklist

Given the complexity of property inspections and market analysis, creating a checklist can streamline the process and ensure no critical steps are overlooked. A due diligence checklist for inspections might include items such as structural integrity, roofing, plumbing, electrical systems, and pest control. For market analysis, checklist items could cover neighborhood demographics, proximity to essential services, average property values, and rental market trends.

Using a checklist helps standardize your due diligence process, making it easier to compare properties and ensure consistency across multiple investments. Additionally, a checklist keeps the focus on essential details, reducing the chances of overlooking critical issues during an inspection or market assessment.

Real estate developer Sarah Brown relies on her checklist for every investment. "Having a due diligence checklist keeps me organized and ensures I don't miss anything important. It's tempting to skip steps when a deal looks good on paper, but the checklist holds me accountable. It's saved me from several potentially bad investments by revealing issues I might have missed otherwise."

Reducing Risk Through Detailed Inspections and Analysis

Property inspections and market analysis are crucial steps in reducing risk and protecting your investment. By understanding the physical condition of the property, you can avoid unexpected repair costs and potentially negotiate lower purchase prices.

Legal and Financial Due Diligence

Legal and financial due diligence are critical components of the real estate investment process, providing insights into a property's legal standing and financial viability. While property inspections and market analysis address physical and locational factors, legal and financial due diligence focuses on ensuring that the investment is compliant, financially sound, and free from legal complications. Conducting these checks can prevent future issues, protect your investment, and help you make decisions based on a thorough understanding of the property's legal and financial landscape.

Title Search and Ownership Verification

One of the most important steps in legal due diligence is conducting a title search to verify property ownership and uncover any existing claims or liens against the property. A title search ensures that the seller has a clear and rightful claim to sell the property, free of any legal encumbrances that could impact your ownership rights. Unresolved liens or disputes, such as unpaid property taxes or contractor liens, can transfer to the new owner, leading to costly and time-consuming legal issues.

Real estate attorney Lisa Harmon explains the importance of title verification: "A clear title is essential. I've seen cases where investors purchased properties with hidden liens, only to end up paying thousands to clear the debt. A thorough title search prevents these issues and ensures you're buying a property with a clean legal history." Engaging a title company or attorney to handle the title search provides an additional layer of protection, as they can identify and address potential issues before closing.

Title insurance is also worth considering, as it protects against future claims on the property. This insurance covers any undiscovered claims or title defects that may arise after the purchase, providing peace of mind and financial security for the investor.

Zoning, Permits, and Regulatory Compliance

Understanding a property's zoning regulations and permit history is another essential aspect of legal due diligence. Zoning laws dictate the types of activities that can occur on the property, which can impact its intended use. For example, a property zoned for residential use cannot legally be converted into commercial space without rezoning approval. Knowing the zoning regulations ahead of time allows you to ensure the property aligns with your investment plans.

Checking for building permits and code compliance is equally important. Properties with unpermitted renovations or code violations can be costly to bring up to standard, and some municipalities may issue fines or require the removal of unapproved structures. Real estate developer Martin Reyes stresses the importance of reviewing a property's permit history: "A property might look like a great deal, but if there are unpermitted additions, it can turn into a nightmare. I make sure every improvement has the proper permits before moving forward."

Reviewing zoning and permit details is particularly crucial for investors planning to make changes to the property, as any desired renovations must comply with local regulations. Consulting with local zoning authorities or a land use attorney can provide insights into any restrictions or processes required for rezoning or permitting.

Financial Feasibility and Tax Implications

Financial due diligence goes beyond simply assessing the property's cash flow and ROI; it involves examining the long-term financial viability of the investment, including tax implications. Property taxes, income tax, capital gains tax, and possible depreciation benefits all influence the overall profitability of a real estate investment. Understanding these factors helps you create a more accurate financial projection and plan for any tax obligations associated with the property.

Accountant and real estate advisor Emily Chen emphasizes the importance of tax planning in investment analysis. "Many investors focus solely on rental income but overlook the impact of property taxes and other expenses. A thorough financial review provides a complete picture, allowing you to assess if the investment aligns with your goals." By consulting a tax advisor, you can evaluate potential deductions, credits, and other tax benefits associated with real estate investments, enabling you to maximize after-tax returns.

It's also essential to verify the financial stability of the property itself. For rental properties, this may involve reviewing rental history, vacancy rates, and tenant payment records. For commercial properties, you'll want to assess tenant leases, including lease duration, renewal terms, and any clauses that could affect income stability. Understanding the property's financial health allows you to make an informed decision and reduces the risk of unforeseen expenses.

Ensuring Legal and Financial Security in Real Estate

Legal and financial due diligence provides a safeguard against potential issues that could threaten the viability of your investment. By conducting a thorough title search, confirming zoning compliance, and examining financial feasibility, you protect yourself from hidden legal liabilities and ensure the property meets your financial expectations.

Investing in real estate involves more than just finding a promising property; it requires a deep understanding of the legal and financial landscape to make informed, confident decisions.

Developing a Risk Management Plan

In real estate investing, even the most promising properties come with inherent risks. Developing a risk management plan allows you to identify, assess, and address potential challenges before they impact your investment. By proactively planning for risks such as market volatility, tenant issues, and unexpected property expenses, you can safeguard your portfolio and ensure steady returns, even in uncertain conditions. A well-rounded risk management plan incorporates insurance, diversification, and contingency funds to provide a buffer against the unforeseen.

Identifying Common Risks in Real Estate

Real estate investments are exposed to various types of risks, including market risk, tenant risk, and property-specific risks. Market risk is tied to economic conditions and includes factors like interest rates, unemployment, and local real estate demand. A downturn in the market can decrease property values and rental demand, impacting both property appreciation and cash flow. Understanding the market's cyclical nature allows investors to anticipate and prepare for potential downturns.

Tenant risk is a concern for rental properties, as tenant reliability directly affects income. Vacancies, tenant turnover, and late payments can disrupt cash flow and increase operational costs. Screening tenants, setting clear lease terms, and having a reliable property management system are essential strategies for minimizing tenant-related risks.

Property-specific risks involve potential issues with the property itself, such as maintenance costs, structural problems, or unexpected repairs. These risks can be mitigated through thorough inspections, regular upkeep, and setting aside contingency funds for emergencies. As seasoned investor Linda Torres notes, "Unexpected repairs can eat into profits, especially if you're not prepared. I allocate a portion of my rental income into a reserve fund for maintenance, which helps keep my cash flow stable."

Using Insurance as a Safety Net

Insurance is a critical component of any risk management plan. By insuring your property, you protect it against a range of potential issues, from natural disasters to liability claims. Basic property insurance covers damages caused by events like fire, theft, and severe weather. However, in areas prone to specific risks, such as flooding or earthquakes, additional coverage may be necessary.

For rental properties, landlord insurance provides coverage for damages, as well as liability protection in case tenants or visitors experience injuries on the property. Liability insurance is particularly important, as it shields you from costly legal battles in the event of a lawsuit. For instance, if a tenant sustains an injury due to a structural issue, landlord insurance can cover legal expenses and settlements.

Real estate developer Jason Li advocates for comprehensive insurance coverage: "Insurance might seem like an added expense, but it's one of the best investments you can make. It protects both your property and your finances. I've seen too many investors get hit with major expenses that could have been avoided with proper coverage." By maintaining sufficient insurance, you safeguard your investment and protect yourself from the financial impact of unexpected events.

Diversification and Contingency Planning

Diversification is a proven strategy for reducing risk in any investment portfolio, and real estate is no exception. By diversifying your holdings across different property types (e.g., residential, commercial, and industrial) or geographic locations, you minimize the impact of a downturn in any one market or sector. For example, if the residential market experiences a slowdown, commercial properties may still perform well, providing balance and stability to your portfolio.

Additionally, contingency planning is essential for preparing for unexpected costs or market shifts. Setting up a reserve fund—a pool of cash dedicated to covering emergencies or temporary cash flow shortages—ensures you're prepared for expenses like major repairs, tenant vacancies, or other disruptions. Many investors set aside 5-10% of monthly rental income for this purpose, building a financial buffer that can help them weather short-term challenges.

Investor Ana Garcia shares her approach to contingency planning: "I keep a reserve fund for each property, and it's saved me more than once. Last year, when a property needed a new roof, I was able to handle it without dipping into personal funds. Having that buffer gives me peace of mind and keeps my investments steady." A contingency fund allows you to manage property-related surprises without compromising cash flow or profitability.

Creating a Resilient Investment Strategy

A strong risk management plan does more than protect your investments—it allows you to invest with confidence. By understanding the risks associated with each property, securing insurance coverage, diversifying holdings, and setting up contingency funds, you create a framework that keeps your investments stable and resilient, even in challenging times. Risk management is about preparation, not fear; it's a proactive approach that ensures you're ready for whatever the market or property throws your way.

With a comprehensive risk management plan, you position yourself to handle uncertainties effectively, preserving the financial health of your portfolio and securing long-term growth.

By taking these steps, you can pursue real estate opportunities with the assurance that your investments are safeguarded against potential disruptions, creating a solid foundation for continued success in real estate investing.

Chapter 8: Marketing in Real Estate

Building a Strong Brand and Online Presence
In today's real estate market, a strong brand and a professional online presence are essential for standing out and building trust with potential clients. Branding goes beyond a logo or tagline; it encompasses the values, expertise, and image that clients associate with your business. A well-developed brand can convey reliability, professionalism, and market expertise, making it easier to attract leads and differentiate yourself from competitors. Establishing a cohesive online presence across multiple platforms reinforces this brand, allowing clients to connect with you more easily and view your work and testimonials.

Creating a Cohesive Brand Identity

A strong brand begins with a clear and cohesive identity that reflects who you are as a real estate professional and what you offer. Your brand identity should be consistent in all visual and written materials, from your logo and color scheme to the language and tone used in communications. Start by defining your brand's core message: what do you want clients to remember about you? Whether it's exceptional customer service, niche expertise, or a commitment to integrity, this message should be central to your branding efforts.

Developing a logo and choosing a color scheme that aligns with this message can help create a memorable and professional image. For example, a luxury real estate agent may use elegant typography and a classic color palette to convey sophistication, while an agent specializing in family-friendly neighborhoods might use warm colors and friendly visuals to communicate approachability.

Real estate agent Susan Keller shares how her brand identity has helped attract the right clients. "I focus on historic properties, so my branding is classic and refined, with a logo that reflects architectural heritage. Clients who love these types of homes immediately connect with the brand, which helps build trust even before we meet." Consistency is key—when your brand elements align with your target market, clients are more likely to remember you and feel confident in your expertise.

Building a Professional Website

Your website serves as the foundation of your online presence and is often the first point of contact for potential clients. A professional, user-friendly website should showcase your services, experience, and properties while making it easy for visitors to reach out to you. Key features include a visually appealing homepage, an "About" section that highlights your background and expertise, listings of current properties, client testimonials, and a contact form.

SEO (Search Engine Optimization) is also an essential aspect of website development. By optimizing your website with relevant keywords, you increase the chances of appearing in search engine results when clients look for real estate services in your area. Blogging about local market trends, property tips, or neighborhood insights can further boost SEO while positioning you as an authority in the field.

Experienced agent Marcus Hill underscores the importance of a strong website: "My website is my digital storefront. I invested in a clean design, high-quality photos, and easy navigation. It's also optimized for mobile because that's how most people browse. My website helps clients get a feel for who I am and what I can offer, even before they contact me." A well-maintained website that's regularly updated with fresh content and new listings reflects a commitment to professionalism and helps build credibility.

Engaging on Social Media and Managing Online Reviews

Social media platforms like Facebook, Instagram, and LinkedIn are essential for connecting with clients, showcasing properties, and sharing insights into your work and local market. Each platform offers unique opportunities: Facebook is ideal for sharing listings and community events, Instagram excels at visual storytelling, and LinkedIn is valuable for building professional credibility and connecting with industry contacts.

To make the most of social media, consistency is crucial. Posting regularly, engaging with followers, and responding to messages in a timely manner shows clients that you're active and accessible. High-quality photos, videos, and virtual tours can make your posts more engaging and highlight your listings more effectively. Sharing market updates or neighborhood highlights also positions you as an informed and helpful resource, encouraging followers to turn to you when they're ready to buy or sell.

In addition to social media, online reviews are a significant part of your digital footprint. Platforms like Google My Business, Zillow, and Yelp allow past clients to share their experiences, offering social proof to prospective clients. Positive reviews enhance your credibility, while addressing any negative feedback professionally demonstrates your commitment to client satisfaction.

Realtor Linda Martinez emphasizes the role of online reviews in her business. "A lot of my clients come to me because they've read reviews on Google and Zillow. I encourage satisfied clients to leave feedback, and I respond to every review, even if it's just a thank-you. It shows I value their opinions and am dedicated to providing excellent service." Actively managing your online reviews by encouraging positive feedback and addressing any concerns builds trust and reinforces your brand.

Creating a Memorable and Trustworthy Brand

Building a brand and online presence that resonates with clients requires thought, consistency, and an ongoing commitment to quality. By establishing a cohesive brand identity, investing in a professional website, and engaging actively on social media, you create a foundation for client trust and loyalty. In a competitive real estate market, a well-developed brand and a strong online presence set you apart, making it easier for clients to recognize, remember, and reach out to you when they're ready to make a move.

Utilizing Digital Marketing Channels Effectively

Digital marketing has revolutionized the real estate industry, offering numerous ways to reach potential clients, showcase properties, and build relationships—all online. With social media, email marketing, and online advertising, real estate professionals can connect with a larger audience more effectively than ever before. By understanding how to use these digital channels strategically, you can enhance your visibility, attract qualified leads, and nurture relationships that lead to sales.

Leveraging Social Media Platforms

Social media platforms like Facebook, Instagram, and LinkedIn are indispensable tools for real estate marketing. Each platform has its strengths, and using them in tandem allows you to engage with a broad audience while tailoring your content to different user groups. For example, Facebook is excellent for sharing listings, market updates, and local community news, while Instagram is more visually focused and ideal for showcasing property photos, videos, and behind-the-scenes content. LinkedIn, on the other hand, serves as a professional platform for connecting with industry contacts and establishing credibility.

Facebook allows real estate agents to join local groups, participate in discussions, and engage with community members. Posting listings, neighborhood information, and upcoming open house events can drive interest in your properties and expand your local reach. Instagram's visual nature is perfect for creating engaging content that highlights the aesthetics of properties, including virtual tours, drone shots, and interior design features. By using stories and reels, agents can give followers an immersive look at new listings or home-buying tips, fostering a more personal connection.

LinkedIn helps real estate professionals connect with other industry players, from lenders and appraisers to property developers. It's a platform for building authority, sharing market insights, and networking with professionals who can offer referrals or collaborate on projects. Consistently posting market analyses or thought leadership pieces can establish you as a knowledgeable resource, enhancing your credibility with both clients and peers.

Realtor Katie Thompson explains her approach: "Social media is one of my top marketing tools. I create content that's helpful and engaging, like home staging tips and local event highlights. By staying active and responding to comments, I've built a following that trusts me for advice and turns to me when they're ready to buy or sell." Leveraging social media platforms allows agents to connect with clients on a more personal level, creating familiarity and trust that leads to long-term relationships.

Email Marketing for Consistent Client Engagement

Email marketing remains one of the most effective channels for real estate professionals to stay in touch with clients and nurture leads. Through targeted email campaigns, you can share listings, market insights, and personalized recommendations directly with your audience, keeping your brand top-of-mind. Segmenting your email list allows you to tailor messages for specific client groups, such as first-time buyers, investors, or clients interested in luxury properties, making your emails more relevant and engaging.

A regular newsletter is a valuable tool for staying connected with clients, even when they're not actively looking to buy or sell. A monthly or quarterly newsletter can include market updates, featured listings, tips for home maintenance, and community news. This type of content not only positions you as a knowledgeable resource but also provides ongoing value to your clients, encouraging them to reach out when they're ready to make a move.

Automated email campaigns, triggered by user behavior or actions on your website, can further enhance engagement. For instance, if a potential buyer views a specific listing on your website, an automated follow-up email can provide additional details about the property or suggest similar listings. This personalized approach makes clients feel valued and keeps them engaged with your brand.

Broker Sarah Green shares how email marketing has supported her business: "I use email to keep in touch with past clients and share updates about the market. My clients appreciate the insight, and when they're ready to buy or sell again, they already feel connected. A well-timed email has led to multiple deals over the years." With strategic email marketing, you can build and sustain relationships that lead to repeat business and referrals.

Maximizing Reach with Online Advertising

Online advertising, including pay-per-click (PPC) and social media ads, is an effective way to expand your reach and attract new clients. PPC advertising on platforms like Google allows you to target specific keywords, making it easier to reach clients actively searching for real estate services in your area. When someone searches for "homes for sale in [location]" or "real estate agent near me," a well-crafted PPC ad can direct them to your website, where they can learn more about your services.

Social media advertising, particularly on Facebook and Instagram, offers powerful targeting options based on demographics, interests, and behaviors. For example, you can target users in your local area who are interested in moving, investing, or home improvement, increasing the likelihood that your ads reach potential clients. Retargeting ads, which display to users who have previously visited your website, can help remind them of your services and encourage them to return when they're ready to make a decision.

Online ads allow for precise budgeting and performance tracking, so you can test different campaigns and allocate resources to what works best. By analyzing metrics like click-through rates, conversions, and cost-per-click, you can refine your ads and achieve a higher return on investment. Realtor John Mitchell has seen the benefits firsthand: "By running Facebook ads for new listings and open houses, I've attracted clients who weren't actively searching but became interested after seeing the ad. It's expanded my reach and helped fill my pipeline with motivated buyers."

Using Digital Marketing Channels Strategically

A well-rounded digital marketing strategy combines social media engagement, targeted email campaigns, and online advertising to create a robust online presence. By using each channel strategically, you can attract new leads, nurture relationships, and keep clients informed throughout their real estate journey. In a competitive market, digital marketing gives real estate professionals the tools to reach a larger audience, connect with potential clients, and drive conversions. With a thoughtful approach, digital channels can be a powerful part of a comprehensive real estate marketing plan that strengthens your brand and grows your business.

Traditional Marketing Tactics and Their Role in Real Estate

While digital marketing has transformed the real estate industry, traditional marketing methods remain highly effective for building personal connections, reaching local clients, and reinforcing a comprehensive marketing strategy. Tactics like direct mail, open houses, and community involvement provide a hands-on approach that complements online efforts. Combining traditional and digital marketing creates a balanced approach, ensuring you reach clients where they are and develop connections that translate into lasting relationships and successful sales.

Direct Mail Campaigns for Local Impact

Direct mail campaigns are a powerful way to reach prospective clients within specific neighborhoods or regions. Sending postcards, brochures, or newsletters directly to homes can generate interest, especially among homeowners who might not actively be searching online but are considering selling or buying in the near future. Direct mail is particularly effective for showcasing recent sales, current listings, and market insights relevant to the local community.

Targeting specific neighborhoods with direct mail allows agents to position themselves as local experts. For example, a "Just Sold" postcard can build credibility by highlighting recent sales, while a "Market Update" newsletter can provide valuable information about home values and trends in the area. By consistently staying in touch with potential clients through mailers, agents build name recognition and trust, positioning themselves as the go-to resource for real estate services in that community.

Realtor Emily Dawson finds that direct mail complements her digital marketing efforts. "Not everyone is on social media or checking their email frequently, but almost everyone checks their mail. I use direct mail to reinforce my presence in the area, and it's led to several listings from homeowners who kept my postcard when they were ready to sell," she explains. Direct mail offers a personal touch that digital methods sometimes lack, helping agents make a memorable impression on clients.

Open Houses as an In-Person Marketing Tool

Open houses remain one of the most effective ways to showcase a property, allowing potential buyers to experience the space firsthand and get a feel for the neighborhood. Hosting an open house provides an opportunity for agents to connect with buyers directly, answer questions, and highlight the property's unique features. Additionally, open houses can attract walk-in visitors who might not have planned to attend but become interested after seeing signs or advertisements.

For agents, open houses are not only a chance to sell a specific property but also a valuable way to build connections and gather leads. Visitors who attend may be in the early stages of their home search or simply curious about the market. Engaging with them, providing information, and following up afterward can convert casual visitors into potential clients, even if they ultimately decide not to pursue the specific property.

Real estate agent Josh Carter emphasizes the importance of open houses in his marketing strategy. "I always prepare thoroughly for open houses, from staging to providing refreshments and printed materials. It's my chance to create a welcoming experience and show buyers the value of working with me. I've met many clients at open houses who later hired me to help with their home search," he shares. By creating a positive, informative experience, open houses allow agents to showcase both the property and their personal approach, building rapport and trust with prospective buyers.

Community Involvement and Local Networking

Community involvement and local networking are invaluable for establishing a reputation as a dedicated and trustworthy real estate professional. Attending community events, sponsoring local charities, or joining local business organizations helps agents connect with residents and other local professionals, fostering relationships that can lead to referrals and new business opportunities. By becoming actively engaged in the community, agents build a positive reputation that extends beyond transactions, demonstrating a genuine commitment to the area.

Sponsoring local events, like school fundraisers or community festivals, puts your name and brand in front of a wide audience and signals that you're invested in the local area's well-being. Networking with local businesses and joining chambers of commerce also opens doors to partnerships that can lead to mutual referrals. For example, connecting with local contractors, interior designers, or mortgage brokers can lead to valuable collaborations that benefit both clients and professionals.

Realtor Lisa Chen has made community involvement a core part of her marketing strategy. "Being part of my community has made a huge difference in my business. I sponsor a local youth sports team and volunteer at community events, which has helped me meet people who trust me to handle their real estate needs. Clients often say they want to work with someone who cares about the area as much as they do," she explains. Community involvement allows agents to cultivate strong relationships with locals, establishing trust and visibility that extend far beyond online interactions.

Creating a Balanced Marketing Approach

While digital marketing reaches a broad audience, traditional tactics provide a personal touch that enhances relationships and builds trust within the community. Direct mail campaigns can reinforce brand recognition locally, open houses offer in-person engagement opportunities, and community involvement demonstrates a genuine commitment to serving the area. By blending traditional and digital methods, agents create a well-rounded strategy that appeals to a diverse audience and connects with clients on multiple levels.

Traditional marketing methods remain relevant in the real estate industry because they foster personal connections and build community ties. Combining these tried-and-true tactics with digital marketing creates a holistic approach, ensuring that you're visible both online and offline, connecting with clients where they live, work, and socialize. This balanced approach helps real estate professionals stand out in a competitive market, building lasting relationships that lead to ongoing business and referrals.

Chapter 9: Real Estate Technology Trends

The Rise of Virtual Tours and Augmented Reality

The real estate industry has seen a remarkable shift in how properties are marketed and shown, thanks to the rise of virtual tours and augmented reality (AR). These technologies allow buyers to explore properties in detail without needing to be there in person, transforming the way clients view and interact with listings. Virtual tours and AR offer a more immersive, convenient experience, enabling potential buyers to envision themselves in a property before ever setting foot inside. By adopting these tools, real estate professionals can reach a wider audience, provide better client experiences, and differentiate their listings in a competitive market.

The Benefits of Virtual Tours

Virtual tours have become a game-changer in real estate, particularly for remote buyers or those with limited time for in-person viewings. These tours allow clients to explore a property room by room, often with 360-degree views and high-resolution visuals that provide a realistic sense of the space. Many virtual tours also offer interactive elements, such as clickable "hotspots" that provide additional information about key features, from appliance brands to floor materials. This level of detail helps potential buyers make more informed decisions and reduces the need for multiple in-person visits.

For agents, virtual tours enhance online listings by making them more engaging and informative. A property with a virtual tour is more likely to attract online views, keeping potential buyers on the page longer and increasing their interest. Realtor Laura Hudson has seen firsthand the impact of virtual tours on her listings. "When I added virtual tours, I noticed a significant increase in online engagement. Buyers felt more connected to the property, and many were ready to make offers after a single in-person visit," she explains. Virtual tours have proven especially beneficial for high-end properties or unique homes where layout and design details are essential selling points.

In addition to reaching local buyers, virtual tours expand the market to out-of-town or international clients who might not otherwise consider a property. For example, investors from other regions or countries can tour properties and assess their potential from afar, creating opportunities for agents to work with a broader client base.

The Role of Augmented Reality (AR)

Augmented reality (AR) takes property visualization a step further by allowing clients to see potential changes or enhancements to a property, such as new furniture layouts, color schemes, or renovations, overlaid on the existing space. With AR apps, buyers can use their smartphones or tablets to "place" virtual furniture in empty rooms, visualize wall colors, or even test out different kitchen layouts. This helps clients personalize the space and imagine how it would suit their lifestyle, making the property feel more like home.

AR technology is also helpful for new developments or homes that are in the pre-construction phase. Developers can use AR to show clients what a finished property will look like, providing 3D models that overlay onto the construction site or blueprints. This level of detail can be incredibly persuasive for clients who need a clearer vision of the final product before committing to a purchase.

Real estate developer Tim Blake has successfully used AR in pre-construction sales. "We use AR to show clients the completed interiors and exteriors of new homes. They can walk through the space and see how it will look, right down to the finishes and lighting. It's been a great tool for boosting sales, especially with buyers who have a hard time visualizing a finished home," he shares. AR enables buyers to make confident decisions, even when viewing properties that are still under construction or in need of updates.

The Competitive Edge of Virtual Tours and AR

For real estate professionals, virtual tours and AR provide a distinct competitive advantage. Listings with these features stand out on online platforms, offering a more immersive and personalized experience than traditional photos or descriptions alone. They also attract serious buyers who have already explored the property in depth online and are prepared to move forward more quickly when they see it in person. This efficiency not only streamlines the sales process but also reduces the amount of time a property spends on the market.

Incorporating virtual tours and AR into listings also signals to clients that you are embracing modern, innovative solutions. This technological edge enhances your reputation as a forward-thinking agent who is committed to providing the best possible service. Realtor Jenna Park sees these tools as essential for staying competitive. "In today's market, clients expect more than just photos. Virtual tours and AR set me apart and show clients that I'm using every tool available to showcase their property and attract buyers," she says. As more buyers look for convenience and comprehensive online experiences, agents who adopt these technologies can stay ahead of market expectations.

Enhancing Client Experiences with Technology

Virtual tours and AR have redefined how properties are shown, creating a dynamic and interactive experience that engages buyers from the first click. By making properties accessible anytime, anywhere, these tools cater to the modern buyer's needs and allow real estate professionals to connect with clients in a meaningful way. As these technologies become more accessible and refined, they are set to play an even bigger role in real estate marketing, helping agents create standout listings that attract a wider range of buyers and close deals faster. Embracing virtual tours and AR not only improves the client experience but also establishes you as a forward-thinking professional in an increasingly digital real estate landscape.

Data Analytics and AI for Market Insights

In today's data-driven world, real estate professionals are increasingly turning to data analytics and artificial intelligence (AI) to gain deeper insights into market trends, property valuations, and client preferences. Data analytics and AI provide the tools to interpret vast amounts of information, enabling agents, investors, and developers to make more accurate and informed decisions. By understanding buyer behaviors, predicting price trends, and identifying high-growth areas, real estate professionals can stay ahead of the competition and make smarter, data-backed choices that drive success.

Using Data Analytics for Market Trends and Client Insights

Data analytics allows real estate professionals to go beyond intuition and anecdotal evidence, offering concrete insights based on historical and current market data. By analyzing market trends, agents and investors can determine price patterns, evaluate neighborhood performance, and identify emerging property hotspots. This information helps make informed decisions about when to buy or sell and guides pricing strategies that align with real-time market conditions.

For instance, platforms like Zillow and Realtor.com offer a range of data analytics tools that highlight average home prices, days on market, and year-over-year price changes. This data can help agents advise clients on timing and pricing, whether it's a buyer hoping to avoid a peak price period or a seller aiming to list during a seasonal high. Real estate investor Michael Jansen shares how data analytics have shaped his investment decisions: "Using data to track neighborhood trends and property values has transformed my approach. I know where demand is growing, which areas are appreciating faster, and where the best opportunities lie."

Client insights also play a significant role in leveraging data analytics. By analyzing data from online behavior, such as which properties attract the most views, clicks, or inquiries, agents can tailor their marketing and focus on the types of properties that resonate most with their target audience. Additionally, data on buyer demographics and preferences allows agents to adjust their strategies to meet client needs better, creating more personalized and effective marketing campaigns.

AI-Powered Predictive Analytics for Smarter Investment Decisions

Artificial intelligence, and specifically predictive analytics, takes data analysis a step further by using algorithms to forecast future trends. Predictive analytics applies machine learning to vast amounts of data to identify patterns and make predictions about property values, buyer interest, and market demand. These tools provide real estate professionals with the ability to anticipate changes, making it easier to strategize and maximize investment returns.

For example, some AI-driven platforms analyze a combination of factors—such as historical prices, local economic conditions, and demographic changes—to predict future property values. This can be invaluable for investors looking to buy in up-and-coming neighborhoods or developers choosing locations for new projects. By forecasting which areas are likely to see the most growth, investors can make proactive decisions, often achieving higher returns by purchasing before an area's value fully appreciates.

Real estate broker Anna Liao explains how AI has influenced her work: "With AI-based tools, I can get insights into which neighborhoods are likely to appreciate over the next few years. These predictive tools take the guesswork out of identifying high-growth areas, allowing me to advise clients with confidence." By using predictive analytics, agents and investors can refine their strategies, focus on high-potential areas, and make decisions that align with future market trends.

Leveraging Big Data for Property Valuations and Risk Assessment

Big data, which refers to the vast quantities of data collected from various sources, is revolutionizing property valuations and risk assessments. Unlike traditional valuation methods that rely on limited historical data, big data combines information from multiple sources—social media, public records, economic indicators, and even satellite imagery—to provide a more comprehensive view of a property's value and investment potential. This approach reduces valuation inaccuracies and offers a clearer picture of a property's current and future worth.

AI-powered valuation models analyze factors like neighborhood crime rates, school quality, proximity to amenities, and traffic patterns to assess property value with greater precision.

Additionally, these models can evaluate the impact of external factors, such as zoning changes or new infrastructure, on property values, helping agents and investors gauge the true potential and risks associated with a property.

Big data is also essential for risk assessment. AI-driven models can predict potential risks by examining historical data on market downturns, mortgage rates, and buyer behaviors. For instance, some platforms use data on loan default rates and housing supply trends to assess the likelihood of a downturn in specific markets. This risk analysis can be a valuable tool for investors considering high-value or commercial properties, enabling them to approach deals with a clear understanding of possible vulnerabilities.

Property manager and investor Carlos Martinez uses big data to assess risks in his rental property investments. "By leveraging big data, I get a deeper view of the economic factors and trends affecting my markets. I can see if certain areas are prone to price drops during downturns, which allows me to manage my portfolio with less risk." Through big data and AI, real estate professionals can make smarter investments, identify potential red flags, and take proactive measures to protect their assets.

Gaining a Competitive Edge with Data-Driven Insights

Data analytics and AI have become essential tools in real estate, empowering professionals to navigate complex markets with confidence and precision. By incorporating data analytics and predictive models, agents and investors can stay informed about market shifts, make well-timed investment decisions, and manage risk effectively. In a competitive industry, using data-driven insights provides a powerful advantage, allowing real estate professionals to optimize their strategies and deliver results that meet or exceed client expectations.

Adopting these technologies not only enhances decision-making but also strengthens the trust clients place in your expertise. In a field where information is key, leveraging data analytics and AI allows real estate professionals to thrive, providing clients with accurate, timely, and strategic advice based on the latest market intelligence.

Automation and CRM Systems for Client Management

Client relationship management is central to success in real estate, and automation and CRM (Customer Relationship Management) systems are transforming how professionals build and maintain these relationships. By streamlining tasks, managing contacts, and personalizing communication, CRM systems and automation tools free up valuable time and ensure that every client interaction is meaningful and timely. These technologies not only boost productivity but also enhance the overall client experience, leading to stronger relationships and increased loyalty.

The Role of CRM Systems in Organizing Client Data

A CRM system serves as a centralized database that organizes client information, from contact details and property preferences to interaction history and transaction milestones. By having all client data in one place, real estate professionals can easily track where clients are in the buying or selling process, follow up on inquiries, and provide personalized service. CRM systems allow agents to segment their clients into groups based on criteria such as location, property type, or buying readiness, making it easier to send relevant updates or offers to the right audience.

For example, if a client has expressed interest in a particular neighborhood or type of property, the CRM system can keep that information readily accessible. When a new listing that matches their criteria becomes available, the agent can quickly reach out with a tailored message, demonstrating attentiveness to the client's preferences. Realtor Josh Evans shares how his CRM has enhanced his workflow: "With my CRM, I have a clear view of all my client interactions. I can see what we discussed last, set reminders for follow-ups, and send personalized listings without missing a beat. It keeps my business organized and my clients happy."

A CRM system can also help manage the transactional side of real estate, with features that track contract deadlines, inspection dates, and closing milestones. By staying organized and on top of these details, agents ensure that nothing falls through the cracks, maintaining a smooth transaction process that clients appreciate.

Automation for Efficiency and Consistent Communication

Automation tools work hand in hand with CRM systems, handling routine tasks and ensuring consistent communication. By automating tasks like email follow-ups, appointment scheduling, and reminders, agents can focus on higher-value activities, such as client consultations and negotiations. For instance, automated email campaigns can send clients market updates, new listings, or seasonal tips without the agent needing to manually send each message. These touches keep clients engaged and informed, building trust and reinforcing the agent's presence over time.

Automation is also effective for nurturing leads. When a prospective client signs up for updates on a website, an automated response can send them a welcome email, followed by a sequence of helpful content. This might include information on the buying or selling process, tips on preparing a home for sale, or advice on local market trends. Automated follow-ups ensure that leads stay warm and receive consistent value, encouraging them to reach out when they're ready to move forward.

Realtor Sara White has seen the benefits of automation first-hand: "Automated follow-ups have saved me so much time. I can set up campaigns that keep leads engaged, and when they're ready to talk, I'm top of mind. Automation allows me to nurture relationships even when I'm not directly involved, and clients appreciate the ongoing communication." Automation creates a seamless experience for clients, giving them timely information and responses without delay.

Choosing the Right CRM and Automation Tools

Selecting the right CRM and automation tools is key to implementing an effective system. Popular real estate CRMs, such as Top Producer, Salesforce, and Follow Up Boss, offer features designed specifically for the real estate industry, including property tracking, client segmentation, and automated reminders for follow-up tasks. Some CRMs also integrate with marketing tools, allowing agents to launch email campaigns or post listings directly to social media from the same platform.

Additionally, tools like Zapier can integrate CRMs with other applications, enhancing functionality and creating a custom workflow. For example, an agent might use Zapier to connect their CRM with their email marketing platform, automatically updating client information based on interactions with email campaigns. This seamless integration makes it easier to keep data current and ensures clients receive relevant communications based on their latest actions or preferences.

When choosing a CRM, consider your specific business needs and goals. If you focus heavily on lead generation, look for a CRM with robust marketing automation features. If client retention is a priority, choose a system with tools for managing follow-up and maintaining long-term relationships. Broker Mark Taylor emphasizes the importance of choosing the right tool: "A

CRM is only as good as the way you use it. I took the time to find a system that fit my business, and now it's an indispensable part of my daily routine. It's helped me streamline my work, keep clients happy, and grow my business faster than ever."

Enhancing Client Service with Automation and CRM

Together, automation and CRM systems enable real estate professionals to provide exceptional client service with minimal manual effort. By staying organized, responding promptly, and delivering consistent value, agents and brokers can build stronger relationships and foster client loyalty. These tools transform the client experience, ensuring that every interaction is timely, relevant, and personalized, which leads to higher satisfaction and more referrals.

In a competitive industry, CRM and automation tools provide the structure and efficiency that agents need to maintain a professional edge. By streamlining workflows and enhancing client communication, these technologies not only boost productivity but also empower real estate professionals to serve clients more effectively. Embracing CRM and automation is a step toward a more organized, responsive, and client-focused business that supports long-term success in real estate.

Chapter 10: Managing Rental Properties and Tenants

Setting Up Effective Property Management Systems

Managing rental properties requires efficient, well-structured systems that ensure smooth operations, tenant satisfaction, and minimal stress for landlords. From tracking maintenance requests to automating rent collection, effective property management systems help landlords stay organized, reduce costs, and maintain high standards of service. By setting up the right tools and processes, landlords can streamline property management, enhance tenant experiences, and protect their investments.

Property Management Software for Streamlined Operations

Property management software has become an invaluable tool for landlords, offering features that simplify and centralize key tasks. Many platforms, such as Buildium, AppFolio, and Rentec Direct, include tools for managing tenant communications, tracking maintenance requests, and processing rent payments. By automating these tasks, landlords can minimize the time spent on administrative work, freeing them up to focus on other aspects of their business.

Rent collection is one of the most significant benefits of property management software. Rather than handling cash or checks, landlords can set up online payments, allowing tenants to pay through a secure portal with options for automatic payments. This reduces the risk of late payments, ensures a consistent cash flow, and provides an electronic record of all transactions. For example, tenant Emma describes how her landlord's payment portal has improved her experience: "It's so easy to set up automatic payments. I never worry about missing a deadline, and I know my payment is always on time. It's more convenient for both of us."

Maintenance tracking is another critical feature. Tenants can submit maintenance requests through the platform, and landlords receive alerts and can assign repair tasks to vendors or maintenance teams. This tracking system keeps a record of completed and pending tasks, allowing landlords to monitor property upkeep efficiently. Regular maintenance improves tenant satisfaction and reduces the likelihood of costly repairs from delayed issues. By staying proactive, landlords protect the long-term value of their property and demonstrate a commitment to tenant welfare.

Establishing Clear Communication Channels

Effective communication is essential for successful property management. Clear, consistent communication channels help tenants feel supported and informed, reducing misunderstandings and fostering positive relationships. A dedicated communication method, whether through the property management software's messaging feature, email, or even a phone line for emergencies, ensures tenants know how to reach their landlord for any issues or inquiries.

Landlords can also use these communication channels to send regular updates or reminders about property rules, upcoming inspections, or rent due dates. For instance, a quick reminder about seasonal maintenance tasks, such as HVAC servicing or gutter cleaning, helps tenants prepare and reduces disruptions. Setting clear expectations for communication—for example, letting tenants know that non-urgent inquiries will be answered within 24 hours—also builds trust and ensures tenants feel their needs are being addressed.

In addition to day-to-day communication, some landlords find it helpful to provide a tenant welcome packet upon move-in. This packet can include contact information, instructions for submitting maintenance requests, an overview of community rules, and any other important details specific to the property. Real estate investor and landlord Paul Davis emphasizes the value of clear communication: "When tenants know exactly who to contact and how, it prevents small issues from escalating. It also lets them know I'm available if they need anything, which helps build trust right from the start."

Routine Inspections and Property Upkeep

Routine property inspections are vital for maintaining the condition of rental properties and ensuring tenants are abiding by lease terms. Many landlords schedule inspections every six months or annually to check for signs of damage, necessary repairs, or lease violations. These inspections help identify issues early, allowing landlords to address them before they become costly. Additionally, regular inspections show tenants that the landlord is attentive to property care, reinforcing a sense of professionalism and reliability.

Setting up a maintenance schedule for routine tasks, such as HVAC servicing, pest control, and plumbing checks, further enhances property upkeep. Some landlords choose to include landscaping or other seasonal maintenance in their lease terms, while others make it optional for tenants. By being proactive, landlords prevent issues that could inconvenience tenants and ensure the property remains in excellent condition, which benefits both parties.

Landlord Sarah Martinez shares how routine inspections and maintenance have helped her: "I have a maintenance schedule set up in my management software, so I know when it's time for HVAC or pest control. These small efforts save me money in the long run, and my tenants appreciate that the property is always in great shape." Creating a consistent schedule for property upkeep not only protects the property's value but also contributes to tenant satisfaction, as they experience fewer disruptions from emergency repairs.

Building a Solid Foundation with Effective Systems

Setting up effective property management systems lays the foundation for a well-run rental business, reducing operational burdens and providing a smooth experience for tenants. With property management software to streamline rent collection and maintenance tracking, clear communication channels to keep tenants informed, and a routine maintenance schedule to protect the property, landlords can manage properties more efficiently and maintain high standards of service. By investing in these systems, landlords ensure a seamless experience for tenants and maximize the longevity and profitability of their investment.

Tenant Screening and Lease Agreements

Selecting the right tenants and creating clear, comprehensive lease agreements are essential steps in managing rental properties. A thorough screening process helps minimize the risk of problematic tenants, while a well-constructed lease establishes clear expectations, protecting both landlord and tenant. By investing time in these critical steps, landlords can create a stable, positive rental experience that reduces turnover and potential conflicts.

The Importance of Comprehensive Tenant Screening

Tenant screening is a vital first step in the rental process, as it enables landlords to assess whether a prospective tenant is financially responsible, reliable, and likely to abide by the lease terms. Screening typically involves evaluating a potential tenant's credit history, employment status, rental history, and criminal background. This information helps landlords make informed decisions, reducing the risk of late payments, property damage, or lease violations.

Credit checks are an important part of the screening process, as they provide insights into a tenant's financial responsibility. A strong credit score and a history of on-time payments are positive indicators that a tenant is likely to pay rent consistently. Additionally, landlords may request proof of income to verify that a prospective tenant earns enough to afford the monthly rent comfortably. The general rule of thumb is that a tenant's income should be at least three times the monthly rent to ensure they can cover the expense without financial strain.

Contacting previous landlords is also valuable in the screening process. A quick call to verify the tenant's rental history can reveal insights into their reliability and behavior, such as whether they paid rent on time, respected property rules, and maintained the property in good condition. Real estate investor and landlord Amanda Jacobs highlights the importance of due diligence: "I always check references and previous rental history. It's saved me from several difficult situations and ensures I have reliable tenants. A bit of extra effort upfront can save you a lot of trouble down the road."

Drafting a Clear and Legally Sound Lease Agreement

A lease agreement is more than just a contract; it's a comprehensive document that outlines the terms and conditions of the rental arrangement, setting expectations for both the landlord and tenant. A well-drafted lease provides clarity on issues like rent amount, due dates, maintenance responsibilities, and rules for tenant behavior, helping prevent misunderstandings and conflicts. It also serves as a legally binding agreement that can protect landlords in the event of a dispute.

Key elements to include in a lease agreement are the rental term (such as month-to-month or annual), rent amount and due date, security deposit requirements, and late fee policies. Additionally, it's essential to specify maintenance responsibilities, clarifying which repairs the landlord will cover and which are the tenant's responsibility. Including clauses on property upkeep, such as prohibiting smoking indoors or requiring tenant approval for pet ownership, can help protect the property and ensure it remains in good condition.

Behavioral rules, such as noise policies or guest limits, are also important, as they help maintain a peaceful environment for all tenants and neighbors. For instance, landlords may specify quiet hours or restrict large gatherings to minimize disruptions in multi-unit properties. Including these details in the lease sets clear expectations and empowers landlords to enforce policies fairly.

Real estate attorney Mark Voss emphasizes the importance of a legally sound lease. "A well-written lease protects both parties. If issues arise, the lease serves as a reference point, outlining the agreed-upon terms. I recommend having a legal professional review it to ensure compliance with local laws and prevent potential legal challenges." By drafting a detailed lease agreement, landlords establish a strong foundation for the rental relationship, protecting their rights and clarifying the tenant's obligations.

Setting the Tone for a Positive Landlord–Tenant Relationship

The tenant screening process and lease agreement set the tone for a respectful and professional landlord-tenant relationship. A thorough screening process shows tenants that the landlord is invested in maintaining a stable, safe, and well-managed property, which can attract more responsible applicants. Likewise, a detailed lease agreement reflects a landlord's commitment to transparency and fairness, providing tenants with a clear understanding of their rights and responsibilities.

Communicating openly during the application and lease-signing process also builds trust. Landlords who take the time to explain lease terms, answer questions, and address any concerns demonstrate that they value the tenant's experience. This openness can lead to higher tenant satisfaction and lower turnover, as tenants are more likely to feel supported and respected.

Landlord John Rivera describes how setting expectations early has benefited his rentals: "By being clear about the rules and responsibilities upfront, I've had fewer issues down the line. Tenants appreciate knowing what's expected of them, and I find they're more likely to take care of the property and pay rent on time." By fostering a positive dynamic from the beginning, landlords can create a stable, harmonious rental environment.

Creating a Strong Foundation for Successful Tenancies

Effective tenant screening and a clear lease agreement are fundamental to successful rental property management. These steps minimize risks, prevent misunderstandings, and create a foundation of trust and mutual respect between landlord and tenant. By selecting reliable tenants and establishing well-defined terms, landlords protect their investments and foster positive tenant relationships, creating a rental experience that benefits both parties. A proactive approach to screening and leasing ensures smoother operations, reducing the likelihood of issues and supporting long-term success in property management.

Maintaining Positive Tenant Relations and Handling Issues

Building and maintaining positive relationships with tenants is essential to successful property management. Happy tenants are more likely to pay rent on time, respect property rules, and renew their leases, reducing turnover and vacancy costs for landlords. However, issues are inevitable in any rental arrangement, from late payments to maintenance requests and property damage. Approaching these situations with open communication, empathy, and a problem-solving mindset can help landlords address issues effectively, keeping tenant relations strong and ensuring a smooth rental experience for both parties.

The Importance of Open and Consistent Communication

Open communication is the foundation of positive tenant relations. Tenants need to feel comfortable reaching out to their landlord, whether to report a maintenance issue, ask a question about their lease, or provide notice when they intend to move. By establishing clear communication channels from the start—such as phone, email, or an online portal—landlords make it easier for tenants to connect with them. Responding promptly to inquiries or requests shows that the landlord values the tenant's experience, which helps build trust and satisfaction.

Regular, proactive communication also makes tenants feel more connected to the property and landlord. Sending periodic updates, reminders about rent due dates, or notices for routine maintenance keeps tenants informed and minimizes the likelihood of misunderstandings. For example, sending a reminder about an upcoming inspection with a brief explanation of its purpose can help tenants feel more comfortable, reducing any potential stress or resistance.

Property manager and landlord Jessica Turner emphasizes the benefits of consistent communication: "I make it a point to reach out periodically, even if it's just to check in and see how everything is going. Tenants appreciate the effort, and it keeps our relationship positive. When issues do arise, they're much more willing to work with me to resolve them because we already have that foundation of respect." Consistent communication helps create a supportive environment, allowing tenants to feel valued and respected.

Addressing Issues with Empathy and Fairness

When problems arise, whether due to late rent payments or property damage, handling these situations with empathy and professionalism can make a significant difference in tenant relations. Instead of approaching issues with a punitive mindset, landlords can use these moments to reinforce their commitment to finding fair solutions and supporting the tenant's experience.

For example, if a tenant is late with rent due to a temporary financial setback, the landlord may consider offering a payment plan or a short extension, particularly if the tenant has a reliable history. A compassionate response not only helps the tenant get back on track but also builds goodwill, increasing the likelihood that they will stay loyal to the landlord. However, it's also important to maintain clear boundaries—setting expectations for future payments and explaining any late fees that may apply ensures the tenant understands the terms and can avoid similar situations in the future.

Real estate investor and landlord Daniel Hodge shares his approach to tenant issues: "I've had tenants face unexpected financial or personal challenges, and being understanding goes a long way. I balance empathy with accountability, finding ways to support them while also reinforcing the rules. It's helped me retain good tenants who appreciate that I'm willing to work with them during tough times." Addressing issues with a fair, reasonable approach can turn challenging situations into opportunities to strengthen tenant loyalty.

Enforcing Rules and Managing Boundaries Professionally

Maintaining a positive relationship doesn't mean overlooking lease violations or tenant misconduct. Enforcing rules consistently and professionally is critical to preserving property standards, protecting other tenants' rights, and maintaining a harmonious environment. Whether it's addressing noise complaints, unauthorized pets, or late rent, landlords must uphold their lease terms while balancing empathy with firm boundaries.

One effective way to approach enforcement is to address minor issues proactively before they become larger problems. For example, if a tenant is habitually late on rent, a friendly reminder email can be sent explaining the importance of timely payments and any late fees that may apply. Addressing these issues early demonstrates that the landlord is attentive and enforces rules fairly, reducing the potential for repeat issues.

If a situation escalates, a documented and transparent process helps both parties understand the course of action. Landlords should keep records of all communications related to issues, such as reminders, warnings, or resolution agreements, which can be invaluable if further action is required. Having a clear, respectful approach to rule enforcement maintains the landlord's authority without damaging the tenant relationship.

Property manager Alice Wong has found that balancing kindness with firm rule enforcement has led to more respectful tenant relationships: "I'm always polite but clear about my expectations. Tenants know I'm fair but serious about the rules, which sets a professional tone. When issues do come up, we work together to find a solution, but they also know I'll enforce the lease terms if necessary." A professional, balanced approach fosters respect and clarity, making it easier to address issues without disrupting the overall relationship.

Creating a Stable, Positive Rental Environment

Maintaining good tenant relationships and handling issues effectively contributes to a stable, well-managed rental property. By fostering open communication, addressing issues with empathy and fairness, and enforcing rules consistently, landlords create a supportive environment that encourages tenant satisfaction and retention. These efforts pay off over time, as satisfied tenants are more likely to renew leases, care for the property, and refer friends or family.

A positive landlord-tenant relationship not only makes day-to-day management smoother but also strengthens the landlord's reputation and attracts reliable tenants in the future. By investing in strong tenant relationships, landlords build a foundation for long-term success in rental property management, benefiting both their business and the tenant experience.

Chapter 11: Commercial Real Estate Insights

Understanding Commercial Property Types and Their Market Dynamics

Investing in commercial real estate offers unique opportunities and challenges, largely influenced by the type of property and its market dynamics. Unlike residential properties, commercial properties cater to businesses and organizations, meaning that factors like lease terms, tenant needs, and economic conditions play a significant role in determining value and demand. By understanding the different types of commercial properties and the specific factors that impact their performance, investors can make informed choices that align with their goals and risk tolerance.

Office Spaces

Office spaces are a popular category of commercial real estate and are typically located in urban centers, business districts, or suburban office parks. Office properties are often leased to businesses, ranging from small firms to large corporations, and come in different classes: Class A, B, and C. Class A properties are high-end buildings with premium amenities and locations, attracting top-tier tenants, while Class B and C buildings offer more affordable options in secondary locations or older buildings.

The demand for office space is highly influenced by the local economy, job market, and trends in workplace culture. For instance, cities with a strong financial, technology, or legal sector often see higher demand for office spaces. However, recent shifts towards remote work and flexible workspaces have affected the office sector, particularly in areas where employees prefer remote or hybrid work models. As a result, investors are increasingly exploring adaptable office spaces, such as coworking environments, to meet evolving tenant needs.

Investor Greg Larson explains how understanding these trends has helped his office investments: "In recent years, we've seen a move towards flexible leases and coworking spaces, especially in tech hubs. Investing in adaptable office properties has helped me maintain high occupancy rates, even as companies adjust their space needs." By staying attuned to workforce trends and tenant preferences, office space investors can better anticipate demand and adapt their strategies accordingly.

Retail Centers

Retail properties, including strip malls, shopping centers, and standalone stores, are another significant segment of commercial real estate. Retail properties serve consumer-facing businesses, such as shops, restaurants, and entertainment venues. The performance of retail properties depends heavily on foot traffic, visibility, and consumer spending habits, making location a critical factor in assessing a property's potential.

Retail spaces have faced substantial changes with the rise of e-commerce, which has affected demand for traditional retail centers. However, properties in prime locations or those with a mix of essential services—such as grocery stores, pharmacies, and fitness centers—continue to attract stable tenants. Some investors are diversifying retail properties by including experiential tenants, like restaurants and fitness centers, which draw consumers for services that cannot be replicated online.

Retail property investor Laura Nguyen shares her approach: "I look for retail spaces with a mix of tenants that offer essential services. I also focus on properties in high-traffic areas with strong community engagement. Even as shopping habits change, people still want local access to certain services." Retail centers that can adapt to changing consumer preferences, while offering convenience and a diverse mix of tenants, are well-positioned to succeed in the evolving retail landscape.

Industrial and Multifamily Properties

Industrial properties are highly sought after due to the growth of e-commerce, logistics, and manufacturing sectors. These properties include warehouses, distribution centers, and manufacturing facilities, often located near major transportation hubs. Industrial tenants typically sign longer leases, providing investors with stable cash flow and lower turnover. However, industrial properties can be affected by shifts in supply chain dynamics, transportation costs, and economic cycles. Investors in this sector benefit from staying informed about logistics trends and regional demand for warehousing.

Warehouse owner and investor Jason Lee emphasizes the importance of location for industrial properties: "Proximity to highways and distribution centers is essential for industrial tenants. I've seen tremendous demand for well-located warehouses, especially with the rise in online shopping." Industrial properties near transportation networks and major markets tend to have strong tenant demand, making location a key factor in long-term success.

Multifamily properties, while technically a blend of residential and commercial real estate, are commonly considered part of commercial investment portfolios due to their scale and income potential. Multifamily properties include apartment complexes and rental communities, typically serving tenants on short-term leases. These properties offer a stable revenue stream, as housing demand remains consistent, especially in urban areas with limited housing supply. Factors like neighborhood quality, amenities, and proximity to employment centers heavily influence occupancy rates and rental income in multifamily properties.

Real estate investor Sarah Kim, who specializes in multifamily units, highlights the appeal of this property type: "Multifamily properties offer steady cash flow and resilience, even during economic downturns. People always need housing, so I focus on properties with strong occupancy potential in desirable neighborhoods." Multifamily investments provide reliable income and are generally less impacted by economic cycles, as housing is an essential need, making them attractive for risk-conscious investors.

Aligning Property Types with Investment Goals

Each type of commercial property comes with distinct characteristics, risk factors, and income potential, making it important for investors to choose the type that best aligns with their financial goals and risk tolerance. Office spaces may offer higher returns in urban centers with a thriving business environment but carry higher risk in areas affected by remote work trends. Retail centers can be profitable with the right tenant mix and location but require adaptation to shifting consumer habits. Industrial properties present strong long-term potential due to e-commerce growth but require careful location selection. Multifamily properties provide stable, recession-resistant income but may require hands-on management or third-party property management services.

By understanding the unique dynamics of each property type, investors can make informed decisions about which commercial properties best suit their objectives. This foundational knowledge helps investors assess which markets to target, how to diversify within commercial real estate, and how to adapt to economic and industry shifts. A strategic approach to property selection allows investors to build a balanced portfolio that maximizes returns while managing risks in the commercial real estate sector.

Financing and Investment Strategies for Commercial Properties

Financing commercial real estate is distinct from financing residential properties, with different structures, requirements, and options tailored to the unique demands of commercial investments. For investors, choosing the right financing option and investment strategy is essential to maximizing returns, managing risk, and achieving long-term success. From traditional loans to partnerships and Real Estate Investment Trusts (REITs), each approach offers advantages and challenges, allowing investors to align their strategies with their financial goals, risk tolerance, and available capital.

Traditional Loans and Financing Structures

Traditional loans for commercial properties are generally offered by banks, credit unions, and other financial institutions. These loans are more complex than residential loans, with higher down payment requirements (often around 20-30%), shorter loan terms, and stricter qualification criteria. Lenders evaluate not only the borrower's creditworthiness but also the potential profitability of the property itself, considering factors such as location, tenant quality, and anticipated cash flow. One common type of commercial financing is the balloon loan, where monthly payments are based on a 20-30 year amortization schedule but come with a shorter loan term, typically 5-10 years, at which point a large balloon payment is due.

In addition to down payments, traditional commercial loans often require that the property meets a specific debt service coverage ratio (DSCR), which is the ratio of the property's net operating income to its annual debt obligations. Most lenders look for a DSCR of at least 1.25, meaning that the property generates 25% more income than the amount needed to cover debt payments. This ensures that the property's income can comfortably cover its loan obligations, providing a buffer for investors.

Commercial real estate investor Dan Phillips explains how understanding these requirements has helped him secure favorable financing: "I always make sure my properties exceed the lender's DSCR requirements, which gives me leverage to negotiate better terms. When lenders see strong cash flow potential, they're more likely to work with you on interest rates and loan conditions." A solid understanding of DSCR and other lending criteria can help investors present a compelling case to lenders, securing financing on more favorable terms.

Syndications and Partnerships for Shared Investment

For investors who may not have the capital required for a traditional commercial loan or who want to share the risks and rewards of larger investments, syndications and partnerships offer an effective alternative. In a syndication, multiple investors pool their funds to purchase a commercial property, often under the management of a sponsor or lead investor. Each investor owns a share of the property and receives a portion of the profits, based on their investment. Syndications allow investors to participate in high-value properties—such as large office buildings, retail centers, or multifamily complexes—that would be otherwise unaffordable for a single investor.

Partnerships operate similarly, though they often involve a smaller group of investors who may play an active role in the investment. In a limited partnership (LP), one or more general partners (GPs) handle the property's management, while limited partners contribute capital without direct involvement in day-to-day operations. Partnerships and syndications are attractive to investors who prefer a hands-off approach, as they benefit from the expertise of the managing partner or sponsor.

Investor Maria Tan has successfully used syndications to diversify her portfolio: "Syndications allow me to invest in larger properties without handling all the management details myself. I get to share in the returns of a well-managed property without the same level of involvement. It's a win-win for those of us looking to scale." By pooling resources, investors can access higher-value properties with lower individual risk, benefiting from professional management while diversifying their holdings.

Real Estate Investment Trusts (REITs) for Passive Investment

For those seeking a passive investment option, Real Estate Investment Trusts (REITs) provide a way to invest in commercial real estate without direct property ownership. REITs are companies that own, operate, or finance income-producing real estate, allowing investors to buy shares in the trust and earn dividends based on the income generated by the portfolio. There are different types of REITs, including equity REITs, which own and operate properties, and mortgage REITs, which invest in property loans. Equity REITs are particularly popular, as they offer dividends based on rental income and property appreciation.

REITs are publicly traded on major stock exchanges, making them accessible to individual investors who want exposure to commercial real estate with liquidity similar to stocks. This liquidity makes REITs attractive to investors who may not want to commit capital to a single property for an extended period. Additionally, REITs are managed by professionals, which means investors benefit from expert management and diversified property holdings, often across multiple sectors and geographic locations.

Investor James Miller shares why he includes REITs in his portfolio: "REITs give me exposure to commercial real estate without the responsibilities of ownership. I can buy and sell shares as needed, which provides flexibility. Plus, I get access to high-quality properties managed by experienced professionals." For investors who prefer a hands-off approach or want the flexibility to adjust their holdings, REITs offer a practical entry point into commercial real estate, with the added benefit of professional management and diversification.

Choosing the Right Investment Strategy

Each financing option and investment strategy offers distinct benefits and challenges, making it important for investors to choose the approach that aligns with their financial goals and risk tolerance. Traditional loans offer full ownership and control but come with higher capital requirements and financial risks. Syndications and partnerships provide access to larger properties with shared risk and less direct involvement, making them suitable for investors interested in scaling their portfolios without solo management. REITs, on the other hand, are ideal for investors seeking a highly liquid, passive investment option with professional oversight.

For new investors, starting with a smaller property through traditional financing can provide hands-on experience in commercial property management. Those looking to scale quickly may prefer syndications or partnerships to spread capital across multiple properties. Meanwhile, investors seeking passive income with minimal involvement may find REITs an appealing choice. By understanding these options, investors can tailor their strategy to their unique financial situation, gaining access to commercial real estate in a way that best suits their objectives.

Selecting the right financing and investment strategy for commercial properties allows investors to manage their risk, capitalize on market opportunities, and build a diversified portfolio. With careful consideration of each option, investors can create a strategic path that supports their long-term success in commercial real estate.

Market Analysis and Due Diligence for Commercial Investments

Conducting a thorough market analysis and due diligence is crucial for successful commercial real estate investments. These steps help investors understand the property's income potential, assess risks, and ensure the investment aligns with their financial goals. By evaluating key metrics such as vacancy rates, cap rates, and tenant creditworthiness, as well as performing a detailed analysis of the property's condition and location, investors can make well-informed decisions that minimize risks and maximize returns.

Evaluating Market and Location Dynamics

The first step in commercial real estate analysis is understanding the broader market and location dynamics. Factors such as local economic conditions, population growth, and business activity can greatly influence demand for commercial properties. For example, a property in a growing urban area with a strong job market and increasing population is more likely to attract tenants and maintain stable income than one in a declining market. Investors should examine local trends in employment, industry growth, and infrastructure development to gauge the market's potential for supporting commercial tenants.

Location is particularly important in commercial real estate, as accessibility, visibility, and proximity to amenities often determine tenant demand. For example, retail properties benefit from high-traffic areas with nearby residential communities, while industrial properties perform best near major transportation routes. Evaluating the property's location within its market allows investors to anticipate how well it will attract tenants and retain value over time.

Commercial property investor Tom Andrews emphasizes the importance of location: "I always look at factors like foot traffic, nearby businesses, and ease of access. Location can make or break a property's success, especially in retail and office sectors. If it's not in a prime spot, it can be challenging to keep tenants." Understanding the relationship between location and tenant demand enables investors to select properties with strong income potential.

Analyzing Key Financial Metrics: Vacancy Rates and Cap Rates

Financial metrics such as vacancy rates and cap rates provide critical insights into a property's income potential and market value. Vacancy rate refers to the percentage of available rental units that are unoccupied within a given period. High vacancy rates can indicate low demand or issues with property management, while low vacancy rates suggest a strong, stable market. Comparing the property's vacancy rate to the local average helps investors assess whether it's performing in line with market expectations or facing challenges.

Cap rate, or capitalization rate, is another key metric used to evaluate commercial properties. The cap rate is calculated by dividing the property's annual net operating income (NOI) by its purchase price. This percentage represents the expected rate of return on the investment. Generally, properties with higher cap rates are considered higher-risk but offer greater potential returns, while lower cap rates indicate safer, more stable investments with steady income streams. Investors can use cap rates to compare similar properties within a market and gauge which properties offer the best balance of risk and reward.

Real estate analyst Sarah Reed explains the importance of understanding cap rates: "Cap rates allow me to compare properties across different markets. A higher cap rate might mean more income, but it also indicates higher risk. Knowing how to interpret cap rates in context helps me choose properties that match my risk tolerance and goals." Evaluating vacancy rates and cap rates enables investors to make data-driven decisions, selecting properties that align with their financial objectives and market outlook.

Conducting Property and Tenant Due Diligence

In addition to market analysis, a comprehensive due diligence process is essential to assess the property's physical condition, lease terms, and tenant quality. This process often begins with a property inspection to identify any structural, electrical, or plumbing issues that may require costly repairs. Understanding the property's condition allows investors to budget for potential maintenance expenses and avoid unexpected costs after the purchase. It's also wise to review records of past repairs and renovations to get a clear picture of the property's upkeep history.

Lease terms are another critical aspect of due diligence. Reviewing existing leases reveals details about rental income, lease duration, renewal options, and tenant obligations. Investors should pay close attention to lease lengths, as longer leases with stable tenants provide greater income stability, while short-term leases or upcoming lease expirations may present risk. Additionally, understanding the terms of any triple-net leases—where tenants cover property taxes, insurance, and maintenance—can impact an investor's operating expenses and cash flow.

Tenant quality is particularly important in commercial real estate, as it affects income stability and vacancy risk. Assessing tenant creditworthiness, payment history, and business stability helps investors determine the likelihood of tenants meeting lease obligations. Properties with creditworthy tenants, such as established corporations or national chains, are generally considered lower-risk investments, as these tenants are more likely to honor long-term leases. For properties with smaller businesses or newer tenants, understanding their financial strength and business model is essential to gauge the reliability of income streams.

Commercial property manager Lisa Chan shares her approach to tenant due diligence: "Before buying a property, I assess the financial health of each tenant. Reliable tenants mean steady cash flow, so I check their credit history and payment consistency. It's worth spending time on tenant analysis to ensure a stable income." Tenant due diligence minimizes the risk of lease defaults and income disruption, helping investors secure properties with strong, dependable tenants.

Minimizing Risks and Maximizing Returns Through Due Diligence

Effective market analysis and due diligence are essential for reducing investment risk and maximizing returns in commercial real estate. By thoroughly examining market conditions, financial metrics, and property details, investors gain a comprehensive understanding of the property's income potential and challenges. This diligence allows investors to make confident, well-informed decisions that support long-term success.

By dedicating time and effort to market analysis and due diligence, investors protect themselves from unforeseen expenses, minimize vacancy risks, and position their investments for steady income and appreciation. A disciplined approach to analyzing commercial real estate opportunities sets the foundation for profitable, stable investments that thrive in dynamic markets, ultimately leading to sustained growth and financial security in the commercial real estate sector.

Chapter 12: Residential Real Estate Strategies

Identifying High-Potential Neighborhoods and Property Types

In residential real estate, choosing the right location and property type is key to maximizing returns. Properties in high-potential neighborhoods tend to appreciate faster, attract reliable tenants, and offer stable rental income. Similarly, selecting the right type of property—whether a single-family home, duplex, or small multifamily building—can impact rental demand and the potential for future growth. By understanding the factors that make a neighborhood or property type attractive, investors can make strategic decisions that align with their financial goals.

Recognizing Indicators of High-Potential Neighborhoods

The location of a property is one of the most critical factors in determining its long-term value. A high-potential neighborhood typically has a combination of economic growth, good infrastructure, low crime rates, and desirable amenities. Before investing, it's essential to research local market trends and indicators that suggest an area is likely to attract buyers or renters and experience appreciation over time.

Employment growth is one of the strongest indicators of a high-potential neighborhood. Areas with expanding job opportunities attract new residents, increasing demand for housing. Cities with a diversified economy or industries experiencing growth—such as technology, healthcare, or finance—are often more resilient to economic downturns, making them safer investments. For example, neighborhoods near business districts, hospitals, or tech hubs often experience high demand from working professionals who prioritize proximity to their workplace.

Infrastructure development also plays a crucial role. Projects like new transportation options, highways, parks, and schools can significantly impact a neighborhood's desirability and accessibility. Investors should watch for upcoming developments that could drive demand, such as new public transportation lines, major road improvements, or community investments in parks and green spaces. Realtor and investor Jake Sanchez explains, "I look for areas where the city is investing in infrastructure. When new roads or transit options are in the works, it's a sign the area is primed for growth. I've seen neighborhoods transform almost overnight after these projects are completed."

School quality is another significant factor, especially for families. Properties in neighborhoods with well-rated public or private schools tend to attract long-term tenants and buyers willing to pay a premium to live in the area. School rankings, graduation rates, and access to extracurricular activities are all important indicators for investors to consider when evaluating neighborhood potential.

Selecting the Right Property Types

Once a neighborhood with growth potential is identified, the next step is choosing the type of property that aligns with your investment goals and market demand. Single-family homes are often the go-to choice for investors focused on long-term appreciation. These properties appeal to families and individuals looking for privacy and a sense of ownership. Additionally, single-family homes tend to have higher resale values, making them a good option for investors interested in buying and holding until the property appreciates.

Duplexes and small multifamily units (e.g., triplexes or fourplexes) offer the advantage of multiple income streams from one property. These property types are ideal for investors interested in steady cash flow, as rental income is generated from multiple tenants, reducing the impact of vacancies. Duplexes are particularly popular with owner-occupiers who live in one unit and rent out the other, allowing them to offset mortgage costs and benefit from rental income.

Investor Sarah Douglas shares why she prefers small multifamily properties: "With duplexes and triplexes, I can maximize my cash flow and spread out my risk. If one unit is vacant, the income from the other units helps cover expenses. Plus, these properties are still manageable without needing a full property management team." Small multifamily units provide flexibility and stability, making them attractive to investors focused on consistent cash flow.

Understanding the Impact of Local Market Trends

In addition to selecting the right neighborhood and property type, staying informed about local market trends is essential. Market dynamics like rental demand, population growth, and property turnover rates can reveal a lot about a neighborhood's potential. High rental demand, for instance, is often a sign that the area is attractive to tenants, which can reduce vacancy rates and increase rental income. Neighborhoods with low property turnover rates tend to have long-term residents, indicating stability and strong community ties.

Real estate websites and public records can be valuable resources for gathering market data. Metrics like average rental rates, property appreciation trends, and vacancy rates give investors insight into the area's performance. It's also helpful to analyze the competitive landscape—understanding what types of properties are most common and what renters or buyers are looking for can inform your decision on whether to focus on single-family homes, duplexes, or multifamily units.

Real estate analyst Marcus Webb explains his process: "I study vacancy rates and rent trends in specific neighborhoods. If rent prices are climbing and vacancies are low, that's a signal there's high demand. I also pay attention to what types of properties are leasing quickly, so I can choose properties that align with renter preferences." By analyzing market data, investors can make evidence-based decisions, choosing properties and locations that offer both stability and growth potential.

Positioning for Long-Term Success

Identifying high-potential neighborhoods and selecting the right property types is the foundation of a successful residential real estate strategy. By researching local economic conditions, monitoring infrastructure developments, and analyzing market trends, investors can choose properties that meet tenant demand and offer the potential for appreciation and consistent cash flow. With a strategic approach to location and property selection, investors are well-positioned to achieve long-term success in residential real estate.

Renovation and Value-Add Strategies for Maximizing Returns

Renovation and value-add strategies are powerful tools for increasing a property's rental income and resale value. Targeted improvements not only make a property more attractive to tenants but also allow landlords to command higher rents and boost property appreciation. However, effective renovation involves more than just aesthetic upgrades—it requires careful planning, budgeting, and an understanding of which improvements provide the highest return on investment (ROI). By strategically enhancing key areas, investors can maximize both rental income and overall property value, positioning their investment for success.

Prioritizing High-ROI Renovations

Not all renovations offer the same return on investment, so it's important for investors to focus on upgrades that will have the greatest impact. Kitchens and bathrooms are two of the most high-impact areas in any residential property. Updated kitchens with modern appliances, durable countertops, and fresh cabinetry appeal to renters and buyers alike, who are often willing to pay a premium for these features. Similarly, a well-designed bathroom with new fixtures, quality tiles, and ample storage can significantly increase a property's appeal and justify higher rents.

Investor and property manager Laura Brooks explains her approach to kitchen and bathroom renovations: "I've found that a modest kitchen upgrade can make a huge difference in rental income. I'll often replace countertops, add new cabinet handles, and install energy-efficient appliances. These upgrades make the unit feel more modern, and tenants are happy to pay a bit more for the added comfort." By prioritizing kitchens and bathrooms, investors can elevate the overall perception of a property and increase its value without overcommitting to a full-scale remodel.

In addition to kitchens and bathrooms, curb appeal is another area that consistently provides high ROI. First impressions matter, and a well-maintained exterior can attract more prospective tenants and make the property stand out in a competitive market. Simple improvements, such as fresh paint, new landscaping, updated lighting, and a clean, inviting entryway, create a welcoming atmosphere. These upgrades are relatively low-cost but can make a substantial impact on a property's attractiveness and marketability.

Energy Efficiency and Modern Amenities

Today's tenants and buyers are increasingly conscious of energy efficiency, both for environmental reasons and to reduce utility costs. Adding energy-efficient features not only makes a property more attractive but can also provide a significant ROI through increased rental income and tax incentives. Upgrades like energy-efficient windows, LED lighting, and improved insulation can enhance the property's energy performance, appealing to renters who prioritize sustainability and cost savings.

Modern amenities, such as smart home technology, are also becoming popular value-adds in residential properties. Features like smart thermostats, keyless entry, and programmable lighting are attractive to tech-savvy tenants and can set a property apart from other rentals in the area. While these upgrades require an upfront investment, they often pay off through increased rental rates and tenant satisfaction. Property investor Jordan Keller shares his success with energy-efficient upgrades: "I installed smart thermostats and energy-efficient windows in my units. Tenants love the convenience and savings, and I've been able to increase rents to reflect the added value. It's a win-win."

Another valuable upgrade is adding laundry facilities, especially in properties where tenants currently need to go off-site to wash their clothes. An in-unit washer and dryer can be a strong selling point, especially for families or young professionals. While this requires an initial investment, it can quickly pay off through increased rent and shorter vacancy periods, as tenants are often willing to pay more for the added convenience.

Budgeting and Planning for Renovations

Budgeting and planning are essential to ensure that renovations provide a good return without overextending the investment. Before starting any work, it's helpful to establish a realistic budget that takes into account both material and labor costs, as well as a contingency for unexpected expenses. The budget should be informed by the expected ROI of each project, allowing investors to prioritize improvements that will have the biggest impact on the property's value and income potential.

When planning renovations, it's also essential to consider the preferences of the local market. For instance, in a neighborhood that attracts young professionals, a property with a modern, minimalistic design and tech-friendly features might be more appealing. In family-oriented areas, features like additional storage space, fenced yards, and upgraded bathrooms might be more valuable. Understanding what tenants in the area value most allows investors to tailor renovations to meet market demand, ensuring that improvements align with what renters are willing to pay a premium for.

Property manager Steven Boyd explains how he approaches renovation planning: "I always consider the neighborhood and what tenants in that area want. It's easy to get carried away with upgrades, but if the market doesn't support higher rents, it won't pay off. Sticking to a budget and focusing on market-relevant improvements helps me stay on track and see real returns." Thoughtful planning ensures that renovations are cost-effective and market-aligned, maximizing the impact on rental income and property value.

Creating a Standout Property Through Value-Add Improvements

Strategic renovations and value-add improvements can make a residential property more attractive to tenants, increase rental income, and enhance long-term appreciation. By prioritizing high-ROI renovations, focusing on energy efficiency and modern amenities, and carefully planning each project, investors can transform a property into a standout rental that commands competitive rents and attracts quality tenants. Value-add strategies not only elevate the property's market position but also contribute to long-term investment success, allowing investors to build equity while providing desirable homes in high-demand markets.

A well-executed renovation plan allows investors to maximize returns, creating a property that stands out in any market. Whether it's a modest kitchen upgrade, adding smart home features, or boosting curb appeal, each improvement contributes to a higher overall property value, creating a win-win situation for both the investor and the tenants.

Effective Tenant Management and Lease Strategies for Residential Rentals

Successful residential real estate investment doesn't end at property acquisition or renovation—it extends to how well tenants are managed and leases are structured. Tenant management is critical for maintaining steady cash flow, reducing vacancies, and ensuring that properties remain well-kept. By implementing effective tenant screening, setting competitive rental rates, and structuring leases with clarity and flexibility, landlords can build positive relationships, minimize turnover, and enhance long-term property performance.

Thorough Tenant Screening for Reliability

A solid tenant screening process is essential to finding reliable tenants who pay on time, respect the property, and comply with lease terms. Screening typically involves evaluating an applicant's credit score, rental history, income verification, and criminal background. This information provides a well-rounded view of a tenant's financial stability and reliability, helping landlords make informed decisions.

Credit checks give insight into a prospective tenant's financial responsibility and ability to make consistent rent payments. Landlords generally look for tenants with a good credit score and a history of on-time payments. Income verification is equally important, as a tenant's income should be at least three times the monthly rent to ensure they can comfortably afford the property. Additionally, verifying employment status and references from previous landlords provides further assurance of a tenant's stability and rental reliability.

Property manager Amanda Harris highlights the importance of a comprehensive screening process: "A little time spent on screening can save a lot of trouble down the line. I always check credit, employment, and call previous landlords. It's about finding tenants who not only have the ability to pay but who will respect the property and the lease terms." By prioritizing thorough screening, landlords reduce the risk of late payments, property damage, and costly tenant turnovers.

Setting Competitive Rental Rates Based on Market Conditions

Setting the right rental rate is key to attracting tenants while maximizing income. Competitive rental rates are based on a balance between market demand, property features, and location. Charging too high may deter potential tenants, leading to longer vacancies, while setting rates too low can mean missed income opportunities. Regularly reviewing market conditions and adjusting rates accordingly ensures that rents remain attractive yet profitable.

A common approach to setting rental rates is to research comparable properties in the neighborhood. Known as "comps," these properties provide insights into the average rent for similar homes, accounting for factors like property size, amenities, and condition. If a property has recently undergone renovations or offers desirable features, such as updated appliances or proximity to public transit, landlords may be able to set rates slightly above the neighborhood average. Conversely, if the local market is experiencing high vacancy rates, adjusting to a competitive rate can help fill the unit faster.

Real estate investor Mark Thomas shares his strategy for setting rents: "I start by looking at the local comps, then factor in any unique features of my property. For instance, if I've added a new kitchen or energy-efficient appliances, I can justify a higher rate. But I also pay attention to the vacancy rates in the area—if it's a tough market, I'd rather adjust the rent slightly than risk a prolonged vacancy." Adjusting rents based on market dynamics allows landlords to attract tenants quickly while maximizing property income.

Creating Flexible, Fair Lease Agreements

A well-crafted lease agreement is more than just a rental contract—it's a document that sets the foundation for a positive landlord-tenant relationship. Lease agreements should be clear, comprehensive, and include provisions that protect both parties. Essential elements of a lease include rent amount, due dates, late fees, lease duration, and security deposit requirements. Clearly defining tenant responsibilities, such as maintenance obligations or pet policies, reduces misunderstandings and promotes smooth tenancy.

Flexibility in lease terms can also be advantageous. For example, offering month-to-month options or shorter lease periods can attract tenants who prefer flexibility, such as young professionals or individuals in transitional periods. However, longer lease terms (e.g., 12 or 24 months) can provide more stability for landlords, reducing turnover and ensuring steady income. Finding a balance between flexibility and security allows landlords to appeal to a broader pool of tenants while minimizing risks.

Experienced landlord Lisa Moreno shares her approach to lease flexibility: "I generally offer 12-month leases but give the option to renew on a month-to-month basis. Tenants appreciate the flexibility, and I get the benefit of steady rental income. Clear terms make it easy to avoid misunderstandings, and tenants know exactly what to expect." By establishing fair and transparent lease agreements, landlords foster goodwill and create a smooth, structured rental experience.

Building Positive Tenant Relationships for Long-Term Stability

Strong tenant relationships are the cornerstone of long-term property performance and tenant satisfaction. Open communication, timely responses to maintenance requests, and a respectful approach to tenant concerns help landlords foster a sense of trust and mutual respect. Tenants who feel valued and heard are more likely to renew their leases, care for the property, and communicate proactively if issues arise.

Being accessible and responsive is essential to maintaining positive relationships. For instance, responding to maintenance requests promptly not only addresses tenant needs but also helps protect the property from further damage. Regular check-ins or newsletters with updates on property policies or neighborhood events can also foster a sense of community. Many landlords find that periodic tenant appreciation gestures—such as a small gift or card during holidays—go a long way in building goodwill and loyalty.

Tenant manager Rachel Lee has found that fostering good relationships reduces turnover significantly: "My goal is to make tenants feel at home and appreciated. When they feel like more than just a transaction, they're more likely to renew, keep the property in great shape, and even refer friends. Happy tenants make for happy landlords." Positive relationships create a stable, consistent rental experience that benefits both parties, enhancing the property's long-term value and reputation.

Achieving Success Through Effective Tenant Management

Managing residential properties effectively requires attention to detail, proactive communication, and a fair, structured approach to leasing. By thoroughly screening tenants, setting competitive rents, and maintaining flexible, transparent lease agreements, landlords create a welcoming environment that encourages tenant retention. Building strong relationships with tenants not only reduces turnover but also contributes to a harmonious, well-managed property, enhancing both rental income and property value over time.

Effective tenant management is a critical component of residential real estate success, providing a foundation for reliable income, positive tenant relations, and stable property performance. Through clear expectations, fair policies, and a tenant-focused approach, landlords can build lasting relationships that support long-term profitability and growth in the residential real estate market.

Chapter 13: Flipping Properties for Profit

Finding the Right Property for Flipping

Successful property flipping begins with finding the right property—one that has the potential for a high return on investment (ROI) once renovated and sold. The ideal flip property is often an undervalued or distressed home in a neighborhood with strong buyer demand, where improvements can significantly increase the resale value. Identifying such properties requires careful evaluation of the neighborhood, the condition of the property, and the purchase price relative to the after-repair value (ARV). By establishing clear criteria and using effective sourcing strategies, investors can find properties with strong profit potential.

Evaluating Neighborhoods for Flipping Potential

Location plays a crucial role in determining a property's flipping potential. Even a beautifully renovated home will struggle to sell at a high price if it's in an area with low demand or stagnant property values. Therefore, the first step in finding the right property is evaluating neighborhoods where homes are selling quickly and at appreciating prices. High-potential areas often have indicators like rising employment rates, good schools, and ongoing infrastructure improvements, such as new parks, public transportation options, or shopping centers.

Gentrifying neighborhoods—those that are undergoing revitalization or attracting new businesses and residents—can offer significant opportunities for flippers. However, investors should research these areas thoroughly to confirm that the positive trends are likely to continue. Real estate agent Michael Kim emphasizes this approach: "When flipping, I focus on neighborhoods where property values are rising, but prices haven't peaked. Areas with strong demand for starter homes or family-sized properties tend to yield faster sales and good returns."

Understanding buyer demographics in the neighborhood can also inform your purchase decision. For instance, in areas with a high concentration of young professionals, smaller homes or condos with modern finishes may be more desirable, while family-oriented neighborhoods often have stronger demand for spacious homes with multiple bedrooms, good school proximity, and safe, walkable streets.

Assessing Property Condition and Repair Needs

The next key factor in finding a flip-worthy property is its condition. The best candidates for flipping often need cosmetic upgrades, such as new paint, flooring, or fixtures, rather than extensive structural repairs. Cosmetic improvements are generally less expensive and time-consuming, making it easier to complete the renovation within budget and timeline constraints. On the other hand, properties with major issues—such as foundation problems, significant water damage, or outdated electrical and plumbing systems—can quickly eat into profits due to the high cost and complexity of repairs.

To assess the property's condition accurately, it's essential to conduct a thorough inspection, ideally with a trusted contractor or inspector who can estimate repair costs. Investor Sarah Dawson shares her approach to property condition assessment: "I look for homes with solid bones that need updating rather than total rehab. Cosmetic updates allow me to maximize the visual impact without overspending, and they're easier to complete on time."

A key part of this assessment is estimating the after-repair value (ARV), which represents the price the property is expected to sell for after renovations. This calculation helps determine whether the purchase price and anticipated repair costs leave enough room for profit. A common rule of thumb, known as the "70% Rule," suggests that the total purchase and renovation costs should not exceed 70% of the ARV. For instance, if a property's ARV is $300,000, the combined purchase and renovation costs should ideally be no more than $210,000, leaving room for a potential profit once sold.

Sourcing Undervalued Properties

Finding undervalued properties with flipping potential requires creativity and networking. Some of the best opportunities come from distressed properties that are not actively listed on the market or are priced below market value. Real estate auctions, foreclosure sales, and short sales can be excellent sources for distressed properties, often allowing investors to acquire homes at a fraction of their potential value. However, these properties may have hidden issues, so conducting due diligence before purchasing is crucial.

Networking with local real estate agents and other investors can also yield valuable leads on potential flip properties. Agents often know of properties before they hit the market, especially if the seller is looking to sell quickly. Similarly, working with wholesalers, who specialize in finding off-market deals, can help investors access properties that aren't widely available. Real estate investor James Foster describes the value of a strong network: "Some of my best deals have come from referrals. I make it a point to stay connected with agents, contractors, and even fellow investors. They know what I'm looking for and send deals my way when they find something that fits."

Another strategy is to drive through target neighborhoods and look for homes that show signs of distress, such as overgrown lawns, boarded windows, or "For Sale By Owner" signs. These properties may belong to owners who are motivated to sell quickly due to financial challenges, life changes, or lack of interest in maintenance. Reaching out directly to these homeowners, either in person or through postcards, can sometimes lead to a purchase before the property is listed publicly, giving investors an advantage in a competitive market.

Setting Clear Criteria for Flip Properties

Having well-defined criteria for selecting flip properties helps investors make faster, more informed decisions. Consider factors such as maximum purchase price, acceptable repair costs, ideal property size, and preferred neighborhoods. Establishing these criteria allows investors to quickly filter through potential deals and focus on properties that align with their goals and budget.

By identifying the right neighborhoods, assessing property condition accurately, and utilizing effective sourcing strategies, investors can find properties with strong potential for profitable flipping. A strategic approach to property selection minimizes risk and sets the stage for a successful flip, creating the foundation for a profitable venture in residential real estate.

Budgeting and Planning for Renovations

A well-planned renovation budget is crucial to a successful property flip. Effective budgeting and project management ensure that renovations enhance the property's value without overextending the budget or timeline, allowing investors to maximize profit upon resale. From prioritizing high-impact improvements to sourcing materials cost-effectively, thoughtful planning is key to keeping renovation costs in check while delivering a high-quality, attractive property that appeals to buyers. By establishing a clear budget, timeline, and renovation strategy, investors can navigate the renovation process efficiently and avoid common pitfalls.

Creating a Realistic Renovation Budget

The first step in planning a successful flip renovation is to create a detailed budget that accounts for all anticipated expenses. This budget should include costs for materials, labor, permits, inspections, and a contingency fund for unexpected issues. A general rule of thumb is to set aside 10-20% of the total renovation budget as a contingency fund, as unforeseen expenses can arise, such as hidden water damage or electrical issues. Having a buffer ensures that these surprises don't derail the project financially.

Prioritizing renovations that offer the best return on investment (ROI) is essential. High-ROI projects, such as kitchen and bathroom upgrades, new flooring, and fresh paint, can make a substantial difference in the property's appeal and resale value. While it's tempting to consider extensive remodels, it's important to avoid over-improving beyond what the local market supports. If comparable homes in the area don't have high-end finishes or luxury upgrades, sticking to modest yet appealing improvements is usually a smarter financial choice.

Real estate investor Kevin Hart shares his approach to budgeting: "I focus on the essentials first—what will give me the best bang for my buck? Kitchens, bathrooms, and curb appeal improvements are my go-tos. I make sure each dollar spent translates into added value, and I avoid overspending on features that won't boost the sale price." A focused budget, aligned with market expectations, allows investors to enhance the property's value without unnecessary expenses.

Prioritizing High-Impact Areas

Certain areas of a home have a higher impact on buyer appeal and perceived value, making them ideal focal points for renovation. Kitchens and bathrooms, for instance, are some of the most critical areas to potential buyers. In the kitchen, upgrades like modern countertops, energy-efficient appliances, updated cabinetry, and fresh backsplashes can transform the space without requiring a full remodel. In the bathroom, new fixtures, stylish tiles, and upgraded lighting create a fresh, inviting atmosphere. These updates not only add value but also make the home more attractive to buyers.

Curb appeal is another essential aspect that directly affects a buyer's first impression. Simple changes like a fresh coat of paint, new landscaping, clean entryways, and updated lighting can make the property look well-maintained and welcoming. Since curb appeal projects are often affordable, they offer a high ROI and can significantly improve a property's marketability.

Interior designer and real estate consultant Lisa Greene advises flippers to focus on these high-impact areas: "When buyers walk into a property, they're looking for a move-in-ready feel. Kitchens and bathrooms make a big impression, and a clean, well-kept exterior sets the stage. It's about creating an appealing space without going overboard." By prioritizing upgrades that resonate with buyers, investors can make a substantial visual impact while keeping costs under control.

Sourcing Materials and Managing Labor Efficiently

Cost-effective sourcing of materials and efficient labor management are crucial to staying within budget. Shopping around for materials and building relationships with local suppliers can lead to discounts or bulk pricing, which can significantly reduce expenses. Many flippers purchase materials at discount stores, overstock outlets, or online marketplaces where prices for high-quality materials are more affordable. However, while saving on materials is important, quality should not be sacrificed, as poorly made finishes or fixtures can detract from the property's appeal.

Labor costs can also account for a large portion of the renovation budget. Working with reputable contractors who understand your timeline and goals can help streamline the project. Some investors hire a general contractor to oversee the entire project, while others may take a more hands-on approach, hiring individual tradespeople as needed. The approach depends on the scope of the project, the investor's experience, and the time available to manage the process.

Investor and project manager John Smith emphasizes the value of efficiency: "I've learned that every day a project is delayed costs money. I work with reliable contractors who understand my timelines, and I stay on top of each phase to ensure we're moving forward. Effective management keeps things on schedule and within budget." Clear communication, scheduling, and accountability help keep the project on track, preventing costly delays that can erode profit margins.

Planning for Contingencies and Staying Flexible

Even with the most detailed plan, unexpected issues can arise during a flip renovation. Whether it's finding outdated wiring behind a wall or dealing with plumbing issues, being prepared with a contingency budget and a flexible mindset is essential. Many experienced flippers build flexibility into their timeline as well, allowing for a few extra days to accommodate delays without impacting the project's completion date or the intended listing schedule.

Setting clear milestones for each phase of the renovation helps keep the project organized and on track. For example, establishing deadlines for demolition, framing, electrical work, and finishing touches allows for progress tracking and ensures that each stage is completed on time. Regular check-ins with contractors and tradespeople ensure that everyone stays aligned with the timeline, and any adjustments can be made as necessary.

Flipper and real estate coach Megan Lewis shares her strategy: "I always have a contingency plan, both financially and in terms of timeline. If we hit a roadblock, I know how to pivot without blowing the budget. Flexibility is key to dealing with the unexpected in flipping." Having a backup plan keeps the renovation process on course, allowing investors to handle surprises while staying within budget and on schedule.

Achieving Success with a Well-Planned Renovation

A successful property flip depends on a well-planned renovation strategy that maximizes value without unnecessary spending. By creating a realistic budget, focusing on high-ROI areas, sourcing materials and managing labor cost-effectively, and planning for contingencies, investors can enhance the property's appeal while staying on track financially. Effective budgeting and renovation planning allow flippers to create attractive, high-quality homes that meet buyer expectations and achieve a profitable resale, ensuring a successful outcome for the project.

Marketing and Selling the Flipped Property

Once renovations are complete, the final step in a successful property flip is marketing and selling the property quickly and at a competitive price. Effective marketing creates visibility, draws potential buyers, and highlights the home's new features, ensuring the property stands out in a competitive market. From staging the property to setting the right price and leveraging various marketing channels, a strategic approach helps attract serious buyers and maximizes the return on investment.

Staging the Property for Maximum Appeal

Staging is one of the most powerful tools for showcasing a flipped property's potential. By arranging furniture, adding decor, and creating a warm, inviting atmosphere, staging helps buyers visualize themselves in the home. Proper staging emphasizes the home's strengths, such as open layouts, upgraded kitchens, or cozy living areas, while minimizing any perceived weaknesses, such as limited space or unusual layouts. Professionally staged homes tend to sell faster and at higher prices, as buyers are more likely to connect emotionally with a well-presented space.

Even if a full staging isn't possible, focusing on key areas can make a significant impact. The living room, kitchen, and primary bedroom are essential spaces where buyers envision themselves spending the most time. Simple touches, like fresh flowers, neutral decor, and good lighting, can make these areas feel more welcoming. Real estate agent and stager Linda Martinez shares her insights: "Staging transforms the way buyers see a home. It makes the space feel move-in ready, which is exactly what buyers want. They can see the lifestyle, not just the walls and floors."

In addition to traditional staging, virtual staging is an option that can be cost-effective, especially for properties being marketed online. With virtual staging, digital furniture and decor are added to photos, providing a similar effect to physical staging at a fraction of the cost. This approach is particularly useful for smaller or vacant properties, giving buyers a sense of the home's potential without the expense of physical staging.

Setting a Competitive Listing Price

Pricing is critical when selling a flipped property. An overpriced property may linger on the market, raising red flags for buyers and ultimately resulting in price reductions. On the other hand, underpricing can leave money on the table. The goal is to set a price that is competitive with similar homes in the area but also reflects the quality of the renovations and improvements made.

Conducting a comparative market analysis (CMA) is essential to determine the ideal listing price. A CMA examines recent sales of comparable properties in the area, considering factors such as location, size, condition, and amenities. If the flipped property has unique features or higher-quality finishes, these should be factored into the price, but it's also important to avoid pricing significantly higher than other comparable properties, as this can limit buyer interest.

Real estate investor Matt Owens shares his approach to pricing: "I look closely at comparable sales and price my flips competitively. Pricing just slightly below similar homes often leads to a faster sale and can even spark a bidding war, which helps increase the final sale price." Setting a competitive price creates a sense of urgency, encouraging serious buyers to act quickly.

Utilizing Effective Marketing Channels

In today's real estate market, a strong online presence is essential for reaching a wide audience. High-quality photos, detailed descriptions, and virtual tours are standard for marketing flipped properties, as most buyers begin their home search online. Professional photography is particularly valuable, as it captures the property's best features and makes it stand out on listing sites. Investing in professional photos and, if possible, video tours or 3D walkthroughs can significantly enhance the property's appeal.

Online platforms like Zillow, Realtor.com, and Redfin are important for reaching potential buyers. Additionally, social media platforms such as Facebook and Instagram offer opportunities to share the listing with a broader audience. Targeted advertising on these platforms can help reach specific demographics, such as first-time buyers or young professionals, who may be interested in a newly renovated home. Real estate agents can also share the listing with their networks, leveraging connections with other agents and potential buyers in the area.

Offline marketing is still valuable, especially for properties in desirable neighborhoods. Open houses, direct mail, and neighborhood signage can attract local interest, particularly from residents who may know someone looking to buy in the area. Hosting an open house gives buyers a chance to view the property in person, ask questions, and visualize how they would use the space. This can be especially effective for flipped properties, where the quality of renovations and upgrades is a strong selling point.

Experienced real estate agent and marketer Jamie Carter emphasizes a blended approach: "A multi-channel strategy—using online listings, social media, and open houses—ensures that no potential buyer is missed. I've seen well-marketed flips receive multiple offers within days because they're visible and look great both online and in person." Combining digital and traditional marketing methods creates maximum exposure, increasing the likelihood of a quick, profitable sale.

Closing the Sale and Maximizing Profit

A strong marketing strategy positions the property for a swift sale, but closing the sale at the best price requires negotiation and attention to detail. When offers come in, evaluating each one based on price, contingencies, and financing terms allows investors to select the most favorable offer. Cash offers are often preferred, as they streamline the closing process and reduce the risk of financing issues, though competitive financing terms can be equally attractive.

During the negotiation phase, being flexible with reasonable requests, such as minor repairs or closing cost assistance, can help secure the deal without significantly affecting profits. For investors, a smooth, efficient closing process is often as important as the final sale price, as a quick sale reduces holding costs, such as property taxes, insurance, and loan interest.

Investor and flipper Rachel Adams shares her strategy for closing: "When I receive multiple offers, I prioritize buyers with strong financing and minimal contingencies. Once I have a serious buyer, I'm willing to make small concessions if it means closing quickly. Time is money in flipping, so a fast, reliable sale is often worth a slight compromise." Balancing negotiation with efficiency helps flippers achieve a successful sale while maximizing net profit.

Ensuring a Successful Flip with Strategic Marketing and Sales

Marketing and selling a flipped property effectively requires a strategic approach that highlights the home's best features, reaches a wide audience, and sets an attractive price. Through professional staging, competitive pricing, and multi-channel marketing, flippers can attract serious buyers and facilitate a quick, profitable sale. By managing the sale process attentively—from staging to negotiating offers—investors can close the flip successfully, achieving a high return on investment and setting the stage for future success in property flipping.

Chapter 14: Short-Term Rentals and Airbnb Success

Choosing the Right Property and Location for Short-Term Rentals

The foundation of a successful short-term rental investment lies in choosing the right property and location. Not all properties are equally suited for short-term rentals; demand can vary widely based on factors such as tourism, local attractions, business travel needs, and seasonal appeal. By selecting a property in a high-demand location and ensuring it offers amenities that meet the needs of short-term guests, investors can maximize occupancy rates, increase nightly rates, and optimize their return on investment.

Identifying High-Demand Locations

Location is the single most important factor in determining the success of a short-term rental property. Properties in popular tourist destinations, near business hubs, or in scenic or seasonal hotspots tend to attract higher occupancy rates and command premium nightly prices. For example, cities with a strong tourism sector, such as beach towns, ski resorts, and historic destinations, often have a steady flow of visitors throughout the year. Additionally, properties in urban areas near major corporations, conference centers, or hospitals appeal to business travelers looking for convenient, comfortable accommodations.

When evaluating potential locations, researching local market data is essential. Platforms like AirDNA, Mashvisor, and Transparent provide data on occupancy rates, average nightly prices, and seasonal demand in specific locations, helping investors make informed decisions. Local tourism websites, city economic reports, and hotel occupancy rates can also give insights into whether an area has a steady demand for short-term accommodations.

Investor and short-term rental manager Dana Torres emphasizes the importance of location: "I only invest in places with a proven track record of tourism or business travel. A strong local economy and high visitor numbers are key. My rentals in areas with consistent demand are booked year-round, even during slower seasons." Understanding the local market allows investors to choose locations that align with traveler demand, ensuring high occupancy and steady income.

Evaluating Property Features That Appeal to Short-Term Guests

In addition to location, the property's features and amenities play a significant role in attracting short-term rental guests. Travelers are drawn to properties that offer convenience, comfort, and unique experiences that traditional hotels may not provide. When selecting a property, it's helpful to consider the types of guests likely to visit the area and what amenities they might prioritize. For instance, families often look for spacious properties with multiple bedrooms, a kitchen, and laundry facilities, while business travelers may prefer properties with high-speed Wi-Fi, dedicated workspaces, and proximity to transit options.

Properties with unique or high-end features—such as outdoor spaces, hot tubs, fireplaces, or scenic views—can command higher rates and attract more bookings. In popular travel destinations, properties with proximity to attractions, beaches, or ski slopes are especially desirable. Additionally, having parking availability, easy check-in options (such as keyless entry), and a well-equipped kitchen can make a rental stand out in a competitive market.

Short-term rental host Kyle Reed highlights how property features can impact booking rates: "I invested in a home near a lake with a spacious deck and a fire pit. Those features are a big draw for guests, and they're willing to pay more for the experience. It's been a great way to set my listing apart from others in the area." By investing in properties with appealing features, hosts can create a memorable guest experience that leads to higher occupancy and increased revenue.

Navigating Local Regulations and Zoning Laws

Before investing in a short-term rental, it's essential to understand the local regulations and zoning laws that apply to short-term rentals, as rules can vary significantly from one city or region to another. Some cities have implemented restrictions on short-term rentals, limiting the number of rental days per year or requiring the owner to be on-site during the rental period. Other locations may require permits, impose occupancy taxes, or restrict short-term rentals entirely in certain residential areas.

Researching these regulations upfront can help investors avoid legal issues and fines that could impact the property's profitability. Many municipalities provide information on short-term rental regulations on their official websites. In some cases, it may be beneficial to consult with a local attorney or property manager who is familiar with the area's short-term rental landscape.

For example, short-term rental investor Lisa Parker shares her experience with navigating regulations: "I always verify the local rules before purchasing a property. In some cities, short-term rentals are heavily restricted, so I focus on areas with clear guidelines that allow me to operate without constant regulatory concerns." Understanding and complying with local regulations not only protects the investment but also provides peace of mind, ensuring that the property operates legally.

Selecting the Right Property for Long-Term Success

Choosing the right property in a high-demand area with desirable features and in compliance with local regulations sets the stage for a profitable short-term rental business. A well-located property with strong guest appeal and no regulatory hurdles can deliver consistent bookings and positive guest experiences, leading to higher occupancy rates, increased nightly rates, and positive reviews.

By carefully evaluating location, property features, and regulatory requirements, investors can make informed decisions that maximize their potential for short-term rental success. Selecting the right property is not only the first step in building a successful short-term rental portfolio but also the foundation for achieving high returns in an increasingly competitive market.

Setting Up and Managing an Attractive Airbnb Listing

An appealing, well-managed Airbnb listing is crucial for attracting bookings and generating positive reviews. Your listing is the first impression guests have of your property, so it needs to stand out in a crowded marketplace. By investing in high-quality photos, crafting detailed descriptions, setting competitive pricing, and offering desirable amenities, hosts can create an Airbnb listing that attracts guests, maximizes occupancy, and encourages rave reviews. A thoughtfully designed listing not only boosts visibility on the platform but also communicates the unique experience your property offers.

Professional Photos for Maximum Impact

Photos are often the deciding factor for guests when choosing between multiple listings. High-quality, professional photos showcase your property's best features and give guests a clear sense of what they can expect during their stay. Crisp, well-lit images that highlight key areas—such as the living room, kitchen, bedrooms, bathrooms, and outdoor spaces—help guests visualize themselves in the space. Ideally, each room should be photographed from multiple angles to provide a comprehensive view, and amenities like pools, scenic views, or cozy seating areas should be emphasized.

While some hosts opt to take their own photos, hiring a professional photographer who specializes in real estate or hospitality can yield superior results. Professional photographers know how to use lighting and composition to enhance a space, making it appear inviting and spacious. Additionally, investing in seasonal photos or updates after renovations can keep the listing fresh and accurately reflect recent improvements.

Experienced host Maria Chen explains the impact of quality photos: "When I upgraded to professional photos, my bookings increased noticeably. Guests commented on how beautiful and clean the property looked, and they felt confident about booking. Good photos help set clear expectations and make the listing stand out." By prioritizing high-quality visuals, hosts create a strong first impression that draws guests in and builds trust.

Crafting Detailed and Engaging Descriptions

A well-written, descriptive listing is essential for giving guests a complete picture of the property. The description should highlight key features and amenities, address common questions, and convey the property's unique appeal. Rather than simply listing features, create an engaging narrative that describes the experience guests will have during their stay. For example, instead of "1-bedroom with a queen bed," consider a more evocative description like "A cozy, sunlit bedroom with a plush queen-sized bed, perfect for unwinding after a day of exploring."

In addition to describing the property's interior, include details about the neighborhood, nearby attractions, and transportation options. Guests often choose short-term rentals for the local experience, so highlighting proximity to popular restaurants, parks, or tourist spots can make the property more attractive. Be transparent about any limitations or unique characteristics of the property, such as stairs, limited parking, or neighborhood noise. Clear, honest descriptions build trust and help manage guest expectations.

Host and writer Michael Lewis shares his tips on writing descriptions: "I focus on describing the experience—what it feels like to stay at my property. I highlight little touches like the morning sunlight in the living room or the peaceful garden view. Guests appreciate these details, and it helps them connect with the space." A well-crafted description not only informs but also resonates with guests, creating an emotional connection that can lead to more bookings.

Setting Competitive and Strategic Pricing

Pricing plays a crucial role in attracting guests, and it's important to strike a balance between maximizing revenue and maintaining a competitive edge. Research comparable listings in your area to understand the standard rates for properties with similar features, and consider seasonal trends or events that may impact demand. For instance, higher rates may be achievable during peak tourist seasons, holidays, or local festivals, while offering discounts during off-peak periods can help keep occupancy rates high.

Airbnb's Smart Pricing tool can assist in adjusting prices automatically based on demand, but hosts should also review pricing manually to ensure it aligns with market conditions and meets revenue goals. Offering discounts for longer stays or early-bird reservations can attract guests who are looking for value, while providing extra income stability for hosts. Weekly or monthly discounts are particularly attractive to remote workers and extended-stay travelers.

Host Jacob Torres shares his pricing strategy: "I adjust my prices weekly based on occupancy rates and local events. For popular weekends, I raise my rates slightly, and during slower periods, I offer discounts. This flexibility keeps my calendar full and ensures I'm maximizing income throughout the year." A responsive pricing strategy helps hosts stay competitive, attract a steady stream of guests, and optimize revenue.

Offering Desirable Amenities and Unique Touches

In today's market, guests often look for amenities that add comfort and convenience to their stay. Essential amenities like high-speed Wi-Fi, quality linens, toiletries, and kitchen basics are expected in most Airbnb listings, and their absence can lead to lower ratings. Going beyond the basics with thoughtful extras—such as local coffee, books, games, or a welcome guide with personalized recommendations—can set your listing apart and create a memorable experience for guests.

Modern amenities, such as smart home devices, keyless entry, and streaming services, are particularly appealing to younger or tech-savvy travelers. Hosts should consider the target demographic and provide amenities that meet their needs. For example, families may appreciate child-friendly items like high chairs or board games, while business travelers often value a dedicated workspace, extra outlets, and reliable high-speed internet.

Short-term rental host Emily White shares her approach to amenities: "I think about what would make me feel at home, and I provide those things—fresh towels, coffee, streaming services, even a list of my favorite nearby restaurants. Guests love the little touches and often mention them in reviews." Thoughtful amenities enhance the guest experience, encourage positive feedback, and increase the likelihood of repeat bookings.

Optimizing the Listing for Search Visibility

In a competitive marketplace like Airbnb, optimizing your listing to rank higher in search results is essential for attracting guests. Airbnb's algorithm favors listings with high-quality photos, responsive hosts, positive reviews, and active engagement, so maintaining these elements is key. Responding quickly to inquiries and consistently updating the calendar can also improve search rankings, as it signals to Airbnb that the listing is actively managed.

Another effective strategy is to encourage satisfied guests to leave positive reviews. Reviews not only build trust with future guests but also play a significant role in Airbnb's search algorithm. Providing excellent service, thoughtful touches, and a clean, well-maintained property encourages guests to leave glowing feedback, boosting the listing's visibility over time.

Superhost Sarah Kelly shares her tips for optimizing her listing: "I check my calendar regularly, respond to messages right away, and encourage guests to leave reviews. These simple actions help my listing rank higher, and it's kept my property booked consistently. It's all about showing Airbnb that you're a reliable, active host." By optimizing listings through responsiveness, updates, and positive reviews, hosts can increase their visibility and attract more bookings.

Creating a Standout Airbnb Listing for Success

Setting up an attractive and competitive Airbnb listing requires a combination of professional presentation, strategic pricing, and thoughtful amenities. By investing in high-quality photos, writing engaging descriptions, setting the right price, and offering a few memorable touches, hosts can create a listing that not only attracts guests but also leads to positive reviews and repeat bookings. A well-managed listing stands out in the marketplace, drives consistent bookings, and lays the groundwork for long-term success in the short-term rental industry.

Providing Excellent Guest Experiences and Managing Operations

Providing a memorable guest experience is essential to the success of a short-term rental. Happy guests are more likely to leave positive reviews, return for future stays, and recommend your property to others. Beyond good hospitality, effective operational management is necessary to keep the property in top condition and ensure a seamless experience for each guest. By focusing on exceptional communication, rigorous cleaning standards, and efficient turnover management, hosts can cultivate a five-star reputation, increase occupancy rates, and enhance the property's profitability.

Clear and Responsive Communication

Timely and clear communication sets the tone for a positive guest experience from the moment of booking through checkout. Many guests appreciate hosts who reach out immediately after a booking is made, offering a welcome message, confirming details, and providing any necessary information. Pre-stay communication should include check-in instructions, parking information, Wi-Fi details, and a guide to using any special amenities. Being proactive about sharing this information helps guests feel at ease and prepared, reducing the likelihood of last-minute questions or issues.

Throughout the stay, it's important to remain available to address any questions or concerns. Responding to messages promptly—ideally within an hour—demonstrates attentiveness and ensures that guests feel supported. For guests staying multiple days, a brief check-in message after the first night can also be a nice touch, allowing them to bring up any concerns and showing that you are genuinely invested in their comfort.

Host Alex Moreno emphasizes the impact of responsive communication: "My guests appreciate that I'm just a message away if they need anything. A quick response goes a long way, especially if they have a question during their stay. It builds trust and makes guests feel well-cared-for." Attentive communication fosters a sense of reliability, making guests more likely to leave positive reviews and recommend the property to others.

Prioritizing Cleanliness and Attention to Detail

Cleanliness is one of the most important aspects of a successful short-term rental. A sparkling clean property reassures guests that they are in a safe, well-maintained environment, setting the stage for a comfortable stay. Guests expect spotless floors, fresh linens, sanitized bathrooms, and well-kept kitchens. High cleaning standards are especially important in the era of heightened health and safety awareness, as guests look for reassurance that the property is hygienic and safe.

Hiring a professional cleaning service can ensure that every turnover meets rigorous standards, particularly if the property has a quick turnaround between guests. Additionally, creating a detailed cleaning checklist for each turnover ensures that all areas are thoroughly cleaned and prepared. This checklist should cover essentials like dusting, vacuuming, and sanitizing high-touch surfaces, as well as restocking items like soap, paper towels, and toiletries. Attention to detail—such as making the bed with neatly folded linens, arranging pillows attractively, and ensuring no trace of the previous guest remains—enhances the property's appeal and leaves a lasting impression.

Host Emma Lee explains her approach to cleanliness: "I treat my property like a five-star hotel. Every surface is cleaned, every towel is fresh, and I go through a checklist before every new guest arrives. Guests often comment on how spotless it is, which leads to great reviews and repeat bookings." A commitment to cleanliness not only earns five-star ratings but also establishes a reputation for quality that keeps the property in demand.

Efficient Turnover and Operations Management

Streamlining operations between guest stays is critical to running a successful short-term rental, especially during high-demand periods when there may be little time between checkout and the next check-in. Establishing a structured turnover process helps ensure that each guest arrives to a property that feels fresh and ready. This process includes cleaning, restocking essentials, and inspecting the property for any maintenance needs.

Many hosts rely on a reliable cleaning team who can execute quick, thorough turnovers and are familiar with the property's unique needs. Communication with the cleaning team is essential, particularly for scheduling and alerting them to any specific guest requests or areas that need extra attention. For hosts with multiple properties or high guest turnover, property management software can assist in coordinating cleaning schedules, tracking bookings, and managing inventory of essentials like toiletries, linens, and kitchen supplies.

Maintaining a small inventory of commonly needed items—such as spare light bulbs, batteries, and cleaning supplies—can also help streamline operations. These essentials allow hosts or cleaning staff to quickly address minor maintenance issues without delay. For example, if a light bulb goes out or a smoke detector needs a new battery, having these items on hand ensures that the property is ready for the next guest without requiring a trip to the store.

Host and property manager Rachel Morgan shares her operations strategy: "I keep an inventory of all the basics and work with a cleaning team that knows my standards. My team and I do a quick inspection after cleaning to make sure everything's perfect. It's that extra attention that keeps everything running smoothly, especially during busy seasons." An organized approach to turnover and inventory management enables hosts to meet high standards consistently, fostering a reputation for reliability and professionalism.

Delivering Memorable Guest Experiences for Lasting Success

Providing an exceptional guest experience goes beyond meeting basic expectations; it's about creating a welcoming, memorable stay that guests are eager to share with others. By focusing on clear and responsive communication, maintaining high standards of cleanliness, and managing operations efficiently, hosts can ensure that each guest leaves with a positive impression. Satisfied guests are more likely to leave five-star reviews, recommend the property to friends, and become repeat visitors.

A commitment to delivering quality experiences not only leads to better reviews but also boosts the listing's ranking on platforms like Airbnb, increasing visibility and attracting more bookings. By investing in the guest experience and operational excellence, hosts can establish a successful, profitable short-term rental business that stands out in a competitive market, driving both occupancy and long-term success.

Chapter 15: Tax Strategies for Real Estate Investo

Understanding Tax Deductions and Depreciation

Tax deductions and depreciation are powerful tools that real estate investors can use to reduce taxable income and increase cash flow. By taking advantage of allowable deductions, such as mortgage interest and operating expenses, investors can lower their overall tax burden. Additionally, depreciation offers a unique advantage by allowing investors to gradually write off the property's value over time, even as the property may be appreciating. Understanding these tax benefits is essential for maximizing profitability and achieving long-term success in real estate investing.

Key Tax Deductions for Real Estate Investors

One of the main benefits of investing in real estate is the variety of tax deductions available. Deductible expenses can include mortgage interest, property taxes, property management fees, insurance premiums, utilities, and maintenance costs. These deductions directly reduce taxable rental income, meaning investors pay taxes only on the net income left after expenses.

Mortgage interest is often the largest deductible expense, especially in the early years of a loan when most monthly payments go toward interest. Property taxes are also deductible, providing investors with additional tax relief. Repairs and maintenance—such as painting, plumbing repairs, and landscaping—are also deductible, as long as they are ordinary and necessary to maintain the property.

In addition to regular maintenance, larger expenses that improve the property or extend its useful life, such as a new roof or HVAC system, are considered capital improvements. While these costs aren't deductible as immediate expenses, they add to the property's basis, which can be depreciated over time, further reducing taxable income.

Real estate investor Susan Collins highlights the impact of deductions: "My rental properties generate income, but the expenses I deduct each year—mortgage interest, repairs, and taxes—significantly reduce my taxable income. These deductions make rental income more profitable and keep my cash flow strong." By staying organized and tracking all eligible expenses, investors can maximize deductions and improve the profitability of their properties.

Depreciation: A Unique Benefit for Real Estate Investors

Depreciation is a non-cash deduction that allows investors to spread out the cost of a rental property over its useful life, typically 27.5 years for residential properties and 39 years for commercial properties. This means that, each year, investors can deduct a portion of the property's cost basis from their taxable income, even if the property is appreciating in market value.

The calculation of depreciation begins with the property's cost basis, which includes the purchase price and certain closing costs but excludes the value of the land. For instance, if a residential property's cost basis is $275,000, the annual depreciation deduction would be approximately $10,000 ($275,000 ÷ 27.5 years). This deduction reduces taxable income without requiring any actual out-of-pocket expenses, creating a substantial tax advantage for real estate investors.

Depreciation can result in significant tax savings over time, particularly for high-income investors or those with multiple properties. However, it's important to note that when the property is sold, depreciation recapture taxes apply. This means that the IRS taxes the depreciation deductions taken over the years at a rate of up to 25%. Despite this, the ability to defer these taxes can enhance cash flow and help investors reinvest in additional properties.

Investor Michael Wong shares how depreciation has boosted his cash flow: "Depreciation is one of the biggest advantages of real estate. It's a paper expense, but it reduces my taxable income every year, allowing me to keep more of the cash I earn from my rentals. Even though I'll face recapture eventually, the upfront savings are well worth it." By strategically using depreciation, investors can benefit from reduced taxes while building equity and cash flow.

Maximizing Deductions and Depreciation through Accurate Recordkeeping

To fully leverage deductions and depreciation, meticulous recordkeeping is essential. Investors should keep detailed records of all property-related expenses, receipts, and invoices to substantiate deductions in case of an IRS audit. Documentation should include mortgage interest statements, property tax bills, insurance policies, and repair receipts, as well as proof of any capital improvements, such as receipts for new appliances or renovations.

Depreciation calculations are often handled by tax professionals, who can also assist in keeping track of the property's adjusted basis over time. Many investors find it valuable to consult with a certified public accountant (CPA) who specializes in real estate to ensure they are maximizing deductions, applying depreciation correctly, and taking advantage of all available tax breaks. Using tax software or property management tools can also streamline recordkeeping and simplify tax reporting.

Real estate tax advisor Lisa Martin explains the importance of organized records: "The more accurate your records, the better you can maximize deductions without issues. Keeping a well-documented trail of expenses and depreciation helps investors make the most of tax benefits while staying compliant." Good recordkeeping not only reduces tax liability but also provides a clear financial picture of the property's performance over time.

Achieving Tax Efficiency with Deductions and Depreciation

Tax deductions and depreciation offer real estate investors significant opportunities to reduce their taxable income and improve cash flow. By understanding which expenses are deductible and how depreciation impacts tax liability, investors can make informed decisions that enhance the financial performance of their properties. Accurate recordkeeping and consultation with tax professionals ensure that deductions are fully utilized and depreciation is applied effectively, leading to a more tax-efficient and profitable investment.

Leveraging these tax benefits allows investors to maximize their income and reinvest in additional properties, setting the foundation for sustainable growth and success in real estate. Through strategic use of deductions and depreciation, real estate investors can achieve a competitive advantage, making their portfolios more profitable and resilient over the long term.

Leveraging the 1031 Exchange for Tax-Deferred Gains

The 1031 exchange is a powerful tax-deferral strategy that allows real estate investors to defer paying capital gains taxes when they sell a property and reinvest the proceeds into a similar property. Named after Section 1031 of the U.S. Internal Revenue Code, this exchange provides investors with the opportunity to upgrade or expand their portfolios without the immediate tax burden, enabling them to grow wealth and reinvest more capital into future properties. Understanding the process, requirements, and timelines involved in a 1031 exchange is essential for any investor looking to make the most of this tax benefit.

The Basics of the 1031 Exchange

A 1031 exchange allows investors to sell an investment property and defer capital gains taxes by reinvesting the proceeds into another "like-kind" property of equal or greater value. "Like-kind" simply means that both the property being sold and the property being purchased are used for investment or business purposes, so this could apply to residential rentals, commercial buildings, land, or even industrial properties. The tax deferral applies to both federal and, in many cases, state capital gains taxes, which can amount to substantial savings, particularly for long-held properties that have appreciated significantly.

To qualify for a 1031 exchange, the investor must follow specific guidelines and timelines set by the IRS. After selling the original property, the investor has 45 days to identify potential replacement properties and 180 days from the date of sale to close on the new property. These strict timelines require careful planning and coordination to ensure compliance with IRS rules, as missing these deadlines can disqualify the exchange and lead to a capital gains tax liability.

Investor Maria Lopez describes her experience with a 1031 exchange: "When I wanted to sell a small rental property and buy a larger apartment complex, the 1031 exchange let me reinvest my gains without the tax hit. It allowed me to grow my portfolio much faster than if I'd had to pay capital gains right away." By deferring taxes, investors like Maria can maximize their purchasing power and build wealth more effectively through strategic property exchanges.

How the 1031 Exchange Process Works

The 1031 exchange process begins when an investor decides to sell an investment property with the intent of reinvesting in another property. The first step is to establish an agreement with a Qualified Intermediary (QI)—a third-party company that facilitates the exchange by holding the proceeds from the sale until the new property is purchased. It's crucial that investors do not receive the sale proceeds directly, as doing so would disqualify the exchange and trigger immediate capital gains taxes.

After the sale is complete, the investor has 45 days to identify one or more potential replacement properties. During this period, the investor can list up to three properties or, in some cases, an unlimited number of properties if certain valuation criteria are met. This list of potential replacements must be submitted to the QI within the 45-day period, after which it cannot be changed. Once the replacement property is selected, the investor has a total of 180 days from the sale of the original property to close on the purchase of the new property.

This structured timeline ensures that the 1031 exchange process is completed within a defined period, but it also means investors need to prepare in advance. Some investors begin the property search process before selling the original property to ensure they can meet the 45-day identification deadline. Working with a knowledgeable real estate agent or broker experienced in 1031 exchanges can help streamline the process and reduce the risk of missing critical deadlines.

Advantages of the 1031 Exchange for Growing a Portfolio

The primary benefit of a 1031 exchange is the ability to defer capital gains taxes, allowing investors to reinvest the full proceeds from a sale into new properties. By deferring taxes, investors can leverage more capital to acquire higher-value properties, diversify their holdings, or expand into different markets. Over time, this tax-deferral strategy can accelerate portfolio growth, as investors can continuously upgrade properties without the drag of capital gains taxes on each sale.

Another advantage of the 1031 exchange is that it provides an opportunity to consolidate or diversify investments. For example, an investor who owns several single-family rental properties may use a 1031 exchange to sell these assets and purchase a multifamily building, streamlining property management and potentially increasing cash flow. Similarly, an investor might exchange an underperforming property for one in a high-growth area, improving both income potential and long-term appreciation.

Real estate investor David Chen shares how the 1031 exchange has shaped his strategy: "The 1031 exchange has allowed me to scale my investments over time. I started with smaller residential properties, and as my portfolio grew, I used 1031 exchanges to shift into larger multifamily buildings. It's a game changer for anyone serious about building wealth through real estate." The ability to defer taxes and reinvest in more lucrative properties helps investors like David build value and diversify, creating a more resilient and profitable portfolio.

Planning for Long-Term Success with the 1031 Exchange

While the 1031 exchange offers significant benefits, it's essential to approach it with a well-thought-out strategy. Since the exchange merely defers capital gains taxes rather than eliminating them, investors should have a plan for managing these liabilities in the future. Some investors choose to hold exchanged properties indefinitely, passing them on to heirs who may benefit from a "step-up" in tax basis, potentially eliminating the deferred taxes altogether.

Additionally, investors should work closely with tax professionals, real estate agents, and Qualified Intermediaries to navigate the complexities of the 1031 exchange process. Proper planning and advice help ensure that each exchange is executed smoothly and that investors maximize the tax benefits available under IRS rules. By building a network of knowledgeable advisors, investors can execute exchanges with confidence and take full advantage of this tax-deferral strategy.

The 1031 exchange is a powerful tool for real estate investors looking to grow and improve their portfolios without the immediate tax impact of capital gains. By understanding the requirements, timelines, and benefits, investors can leverage the 1031 exchange to preserve capital, expand into new investment opportunities, and build long-term wealth through strategic reinvestment. With careful planning and expert guidance, the 1031 exchange enables investors to reach new heights in their real estate journey, deferring taxes while steadily growing their financial future.

Structuring Real Estate Investments for Optimal Tax Efficiency

The structure of a real estate investment has a significant impact on tax efficiency, liability protection, and long-term profitability. For real estate investors, choosing the right ownership structure—whether it's an LLC, partnership, or corporation—can lead to substantial tax savings, reduce personal liability, and streamline income distribution. By understanding the tax implications of different structures and selecting one that aligns with their investment goals, investors can maximize their after-tax returns and create a resilient foundation for their portfolio.

The Benefits of LLCs for Real Estate Investments

Limited Liability Companies (LLCs) are a popular choice among real estate investors due to the liability protection they offer and their tax flexibility. An LLC separates personal and business assets, protecting investors' personal assets from potential legal claims or debts related to the property. This limited liability is a valuable feature for investors, particularly those managing multiple properties or high-value investments where liability risks are greater.

In addition to liability protection, LLCs offer tax advantages. An LLC is a "pass-through" entity, meaning that the company's income, deductions, and credits "pass through" to the individual owners, who report them on their personal tax returns. This avoids the double taxation faced by C Corporations, where profits are taxed at both the corporate and individual levels. For investors, pass-through taxation can simplify tax reporting and lower overall tax burdens.

Real estate investor Sarah Duncan shares her reasons for choosing an LLC structure: "Setting up each property in its own LLC gives me peace of mind. If there's ever an issue with one property, my other assets aren't at risk. Plus, the pass-through taxation keeps things simple and saves me money." For many investors, the combination of liability protection and tax efficiency makes the LLC structure an ideal choice.

Exploring Partnerships and Multi-Member LLCs

For investors who want to pool resources and expertise, partnerships and multi-member LLCs offer flexibility and shared ownership benefits. In a partnership structure, two or more investors combine their capital, skills, and networks to purchase and manage a property. Partnerships are often structured as Limited Partnerships (LPs) or General Partnerships (GPs), with LPs providing limited liability to certain partners, while GPs involve shared liability and management responsibilities.

A multi-member LLC operates similarly to a partnership but provides the added benefit of limited liability for all members. In both structures, income, deductions, and tax obligations are distributed based on ownership percentages or as outlined in the partnership or operating agreement. This structure allows investors to diversify, take on larger projects, and benefit from shared expertise without bearing the full financial or operational burden.

Partnerships and multi-member LLCs also offer flexibility in profit-sharing and tax planning. For instance, partners can structure agreements to allocate income based on their contributions, management roles, or investment goals. Investor Joe Torres explains how his multi-member LLC partnership has helped his business grow: "By pooling resources with partners, I've been able to invest in bigger properties. We each bring something different to the table, and it's a great way to scale without taking on all the risk and capital alone." Partnerships and multi-member LLCs empower investors to expand their portfolios and share both the rewards and responsibilities.

Utilizing S-Corporations for Active Real Estate Operations

While LLCs and partnerships are typically the preferred structures for rental properties and long-term investments, an S Corporation (S-Corp) may be advantageous for investors actively involved in real estate operations, such as house flipping or property management. Like LLCs, S-Corps are pass-through entities, allowing owners to avoid double taxation. However, S-Corps offer a unique benefit for active investors who pay themselves a reasonable salary, which can reduce the amount of self-employment tax owed.

In an S-Corp, owner-investors can divide income into salary and distributions. Salaries are subject to payroll and self-employment taxes, while distributions are not, creating tax savings if structured carefully. For example, if an investor owns a property management company and actively works in the business, setting up an S-Corp allows them to pay a portion of income as a salary and the remainder as a distribution, reducing overall tax liability.

Experienced flipper and S-Corp owner Lisa Jameson explains the benefits: "My S-Corp allows me to save on self-employment taxes by paying myself a reasonable salary and taking the rest as distributions. It works well for my active business, and the tax savings add up each year." For investors who are actively engaged in real estate operations, an S-Corp can be a strategic choice to minimize taxes while maintaining flexibility in income distribution.

Choosing the Right Structure for Long-Term Tax Efficiency

Selecting the appropriate investment structure depends on the type of real estate activities involved, the investor's financial goals, and the level of liability protection needed. LLCs and partnerships are ideal for passive investments and rental properties, offering liability protection and pass-through taxation benefits. For more active, operational roles like house flipping, an S-Corp can provide tax savings by allowing a split between salary and distributions. Investors should also consider factors like the number of partners, expected income distribution, and asset protection needs when choosing a structure.

It's highly advisable to consult with a qualified tax professional or attorney to determine the most tax-efficient structure based on individual circumstances and long-term goals. Many investors set up a combination of entities—such as forming separate LLCs for each property within a holding LLC or creating an S-Corp for active projects alongside LLCs for passive investments—to optimize tax efficiency across various activities.

By selecting the right structure, investors can achieve significant tax savings, protect personal assets, and position themselves for sustainable growth. Each structure offers unique benefits, and tailoring the choice to specific investment goals helps maximize after-tax income and simplify tax reporting. With the proper foundation, investors can build a tax-efficient and resilient portfolio that supports both immediate and future wealth-building objectives.

Through careful consideration of LLCs, partnerships, and S-Corps, real estate investors can structure their holdings in a way that minimizes tax liabilities, safeguards assets, and supports long-term success in the ever-evolving real estate market.

Chapter 16

Chapter 16: International Real Estate Investments

Researching International Markets and Choosing the Right Location

Investing in international real estate opens up new opportunities, but it requires a thoughtful approach to researching and selecting the right market. Unlike domestic investments, foreign markets come with additional complexities such as different economic conditions, political climates, currency stability, and real estate regulations. By thoroughly evaluating each of these factors, investors can identify international locations that offer favorable conditions for growth, stability, and returns. A strategic approach to selecting markets helps investors mitigate risks and make informed decisions that align with their financial goals.

Evaluating Economic Stability and Growth Potential

Economic stability is a cornerstone of any successful real estate investment, and this is especially true when investing internationally. Countries with stable, growing economies generally provide safer environments for investment, as they tend to have a thriving job market, low inflation, and increasing demand for real estate. Economic growth often leads to urban expansion, infrastructure improvements, and rising property values, creating favorable conditions for real estate investors.

When researching potential markets, investors should look for indicators of economic health, such as gross domestic product (GDP) growth, low inflation rates, and high employment levels. Countries with diversified economies—those that aren't solely reliant on a single industry like tourism or oil—tend to be more resilient during economic downturns. For example, Costa Rica has a growing tourism industry, but it also invests in technology and medical exports, making it an attractive, diversified market for real estate investors.

Emerging markets, or countries experiencing rapid development, can offer high growth potential but may come with higher risks due to economic volatility or political changes. Countries like Mexico, Vietnam, and parts of Eastern Europe have become popular for their affordability and economic expansion, but investors must weigh the potential for high returns against the risks of market fluctuations. Real estate analyst Jennifer Lee shares her experience: "I look for countries with steady GDP growth and low inflation. Even in emerging markets, those signs of economic health are critical for minimizing risks and ensuring property values appreciate over time."

Considering Political Climate and Regulatory Environment

The political climate and regulatory environment of a country play a major role in the safety and profitability of an international investment. Countries with stable governments and investor-friendly policies tend to offer more predictable outcomes for real estate investors. However, investing in countries with political instability or frequent policy changes can pose risks, such as sudden changes in ownership laws, property taxes, or foreign investment restrictions.

Investors should research each country's attitude toward foreign ownership, as some countries impose restrictions on property ownership for non-residents or require specific approvals. For instance, Thailand allows foreign ownership of condominiums up to a certain percentage within a building, but foreigners cannot own land directly. Similarly, Indonesia limits foreign ownership of land, offering instead leasehold arrangements with varying lease terms. By understanding these regulations upfront, investors can avoid legal hurdles and select locations where they can securely own and manage property.

In addition to ownership rules, the ease of transferring money in and out of the country and the risk of political upheaval are important considerations. Countries with strong property rights, transparent legal systems, and stable regulatory frameworks—such as Portugal, New Zealand, and Canada—are often popular among international investors for their stability and investor protections. Political consultant and investor James McMillan explains, "I always look at the country's legal framework for property rights and foreign ownership. If the system is transparent and property rights are protected, it makes the investment much safer and gives peace of mind."

Identifying High-Demand Areas within Each Market

Once a stable country and favorable regulatory environment are identified, the next step is to choose the right city or region within that country. Demand for real estate can vary widely even within the same country, so investors should look for areas with strong local demand, whether from tourists, business travelers, or local residents. High-demand areas typically offer higher rental yields, lower vacancy rates, and better potential for appreciation.

In many countries, popular tourist destinations—such as beach towns, historic cities, or mountain resorts—are ideal for short-term rentals or vacation properties. Locations like Tulum in Mexico, the Algarve in Portugal, or Bali in Indonesia attract year-round tourists and offer opportunities for strong rental income. Business hubs and urban centers are also appealing, as they attract professionals who may seek longer-term rentals or corporate housing. Cities like Dubai, Singapore, and Berlin are known for their appeal to international business, making them popular spots for foreign investors targeting business travelers or expats.

Understanding the local market dynamics within each area can help investors choose properties that align with rental demand. For example, properties in central business districts often appeal to corporate tenants and command higher rents, while properties in suburban areas or near universities may attract families or students. Market research tools, such as online property listing platforms, local real estate agencies, and reports from global real estate firms like JLL or CBRE, can provide insights into average rental prices, occupancy rates, and demand patterns in specific areas.

Property investor Lauren Kim shares her approach: "When I invest internationally, I focus on cities with high tourist traffic or major business centers. I look at occupancy rates, rental prices, and the types of properties that are in demand. Choosing the right neighborhood is key to maximizing returns." By carefully selecting properties in high-demand areas, investors can enhance their rental income potential and reduce the risk of prolonged vacancies.

Building a Framework for Selecting International Investments

Choosing the right location for an international real estate investment requires a combination of economic research, political analysis, and an understanding of local demand patterns. By evaluating the economic stability, regulatory environment, and high-demand areas within each market, investors can make informed decisions that support long-term growth and profitability. A structured approach to researching international markets helps mitigate risks and ensures that investors select locations where they can confidently build and sustain their real estate portfolio.

Armed with a clear framework, real estate investors can navigate the complexities of international markets, positioning themselves for success in diverse, growing regions across the globe. This careful approach not only enhances the likelihood of positive returns but also provides a secure foundation for expanding real estate investments beyond domestic borders.

Understanding Legal and Tax Implications of International Ownership

Owning property abroad brings unique legal and tax considerations that are critical to managing costs and maintaining compliance. Every country has its own regulations around foreign ownership, tax obligations, and property rights, making it essential for investors to understand these aspects before committing to an international real estate purchase. By working with local experts, researching tax treaties, and familiarizing themselves with property ownership rights, investors can avoid costly surprises and ensure that their investments remain secure and profitable.

Navigating Foreign Ownership Regulations and Property Rights

Ownership regulations vary widely from country to country, with some nations welcoming foreign investment in real estate and others placing restrictions on foreign ownership. These restrictions can range from limitations on land ownership to requirements for obtaining specific permits or approvals. In countries like Mexico, for example, foreigners can own land in the "restricted zone" (within 50 km of the coastline and 100 km of the borders) only through a bank trust (fideicomiso) or through a Mexican corporation. Other countries, like Thailand, allow foreign ownership of condominiums up to a certain percentage within a building but restrict direct ownership of land.

Understanding these regulations is crucial for ensuring that property ownership is legally sound and aligns with an investor's goals. In some cases, foreign investors may need to consider alternative ownership structures, such as leasehold arrangements, which grant temporary ownership rights for a specified period (typically 30, 60, or 99 years). Leasehold properties are common in countries like Indonesia, where foreigners can lease land for up to 80 years but cannot directly own it.

Real estate attorney Maria Sanchez emphasizes the importance of researching ownership laws: "Foreign ownership laws can be complex, and they vary greatly by country. It's essential to work with a local attorney who understands these regulations. They can guide you through the ownership process, ensuring that you're compliant and aware of any limitations." By consulting legal experts, investors can navigate ownership rules confidently, avoiding potential pitfalls and protecting their investments.

Understanding Tax Obligations and Double Taxation Agreements

In addition to ownership regulations, international real estate investors face various tax obligations, including local property taxes, capital gains taxes, and income taxes on rental income. Many countries tax rental income earned by foreign investors, which may require investors to file tax returns in the property's country of location. For example, a U.S. citizen who owns rental property in Portugal would need to report rental income to the

Portuguese tax authorities and potentially pay income tax on that income.

To avoid double taxation, many countries have tax treaties in place that allow investors to offset taxes paid abroad against their home country tax obligations. The United States, for instance, has tax treaties with numerous countries, allowing American investors to claim a foreign tax credit on income earned and taxed overseas. This credit helps investors reduce their U.S. tax liability and prevents them from being taxed twice on the same income.

However, not all countries have tax treaties with each other, so it's essential to understand the specific agreements between the investor's home country and the country where the property is located. Tax consultant and advisor David Chang explains, "Double taxation agreements can make a big difference in overall tax liability. By understanding these treaties, investors can take advantage of foreign tax credits and ensure they're only paying taxes once on their overseas income." Working with an international tax professional can help investors leverage tax treaties, structure income tax-efficiently, and minimize their overall tax burden.

Residency and Estate Tax Considerations

Investing internationally can also impact an investor's residency status and estate tax obligations, depending on the amount of time they spend in the country and the value of their overseas assets. In some countries, owning property or spending a certain amount of time there each year can lead to a change in tax residency status, requiring investors to pay taxes on their global income. For instance, in countries like Spain or France, spending more than 183 days in a calendar year can qualify an individual as a tax resident, subjecting them to local tax laws on all income, including income earned outside the country.

Additionally, estate taxes can vary based on local inheritance laws and tax regulations. Some countries impose estate taxes on foreign-owned assets, while others may have exemptions or reduced rates for non-residents. In cases where estate taxes apply, investors may need to plan for these liabilities to ensure that their heirs are not burdened with substantial taxes upon inheritance. Understanding local inheritance laws, including forced heirship rules in certain countries, can help investors structure ownership in a way that aligns with their estate planning goals.

Estate planner and tax advisor Laura Beck highlights the importance of considering residency and estate implications: "It's essential to plan ahead, especially if you spend extended time abroad or want to pass your properties to heirs. Each country has its own estate laws, and early planning can help you manage potential estate taxes or other obligations." Proactively planning for residency and estate taxes helps investors avoid unexpected liabilities and ensures that their international investments align with their long-term financial goals.

Protecting Investments through Legal and Tax Planning

Understanding the legal and tax implications of international real estate investments is essential for minimizing costs and maximizing returns. By researching foreign ownership regulations, leveraging double taxation treaties, and planning for residency and estate tax obligations, investors can navigate these complexities confidently. Working with local legal and tax professionals who specialize in international investments ensures that all requirements are met, ownership rights are protected, and tax liabilities are minimized.

Through diligent research and expert advice, investors can build a solid foundation for international ownership, allowing them to focus on growing their portfolio and achieving their financial objectives with greater security and peace of mind. A well-planned approach to legal and tax considerations empowers investors to take advantage of global real estate opportunities while managing risks and preserving wealth.

Managing and Maintaining Overseas Properties

Owning international real estate comes with unique challenges when it comes to property management and maintenance. Successful international investors often rely on local expertise to handle day-to-day operations, tenant relations, and upkeep, allowing them to maintain the property's quality and profitability from afar. From selecting reliable property management services to addressing currency fluctuations, maintaining an overseas property requires a strategic approach that ensures both efficiency and consistent returns.

Selecting a Reliable Local Property Management Company

For most international investors, hiring a reputable property management company is essential to managing a property remotely. A local property management team not only handles tenant relations, rent collection, and maintenance requests but also ensures that the property complies with local regulations. A professional management company can be especially valuable for short-term rentals, where regular cleaning, guest check-in, and prompt responses are crucial to maintaining positive reviews and high occupancy rates.

When selecting a property management company, it's important to conduct thorough research, focusing on companies with strong reputations, transparent pricing, and positive client testimonials. Many investors also prefer management companies that specialize in serving foreign property owners, as they understand the unique needs of remote investors. Establishing clear communication expectations and setting up regular check-ins can help build trust and ensure the company meets your standards for service and accountability.

Real estate investor Michael Tran shares his experience with property managers: "I work with a local property management company that understands my expectations as an overseas owner. They handle everything from tenant screenings to repairs, and I get a monthly report with updates. It's been a huge relief knowing that my property is in good hands." By partnering with a trustworthy management team, investors can rest assured that their property is being maintained efficiently, even from a distance.

Planning for Maintenance and Operational Costs

Regular maintenance is essential for keeping an overseas property in top condition and retaining its value. Even with a property management team in place, it's important for investors to budget for routine maintenance, repairs, and unexpected expenses that may arise. This can include everything from landscaping and pest control to plumbing repairs and appliance replacements. Proactive maintenance helps avoid costly repairs down the line and ensures a positive experience for tenants or guests.

Operational costs can vary widely depending on the property's location and the type of rental it serves. For instance, short-term rentals may require more frequent cleaning and higher upkeep costs due to higher turnover, while long-term rentals may have steadier maintenance demands. Some investors find it helpful to set aside a portion of rental income each month in a reserve fund to cover future repairs and improvements, allowing them to address maintenance issues without straining cash flow.

Property manager Sarah Lang emphasizes the importance of budgeting for maintenance: "Maintenance costs can add up, especially for overseas properties where local labor rates or materials may vary. Having a reserve fund for unexpected repairs has saved me from scrambling when issues arise." By planning for maintenance expenses, investors can ensure that their property remains attractive and functional, protecting both the property's value and rental income potential.

Addressing Currency Fluctuations and Financial Management

One unique consideration for international real estate investors is currency exchange rates, which can impact both rental income and expenses. For example, if a U.S.-based investor owns a property in Europe, fluctuations in the euro-to-dollar exchange rate can affect the value of rental income once it's converted to U.S. dollars. Currency fluctuations can also impact expenses, such as property management fees, maintenance costs, and local taxes, all of which may be paid in the property's local currency.

To manage this risk, some investors use multi-currency accounts or work with currency exchange services that allow them to lock in favorable exchange rates. This approach helps stabilize cash flow and provides greater predictability for long-term financial planning. For properties that generate income in foreign currency, investors may also consider reinvesting locally or holding funds in the same currency to avoid frequent conversions. Using automated transfer services can further simplify the process, ensuring that rental income is converted and deposited into the investor's primary account with minimal hassle.

Investor David Chen explains his approach to currency management: "Since my property is in Mexico, I use a multi-currency account to hold pesos when the exchange rate is favorable. I also reinvest part of my rental income locally, which reduces the need to convert money often. This way, I avoid the impact of currency fluctuations on my income." By taking a proactive approach to currency management, investors can mitigate the effects of fluctuating exchange rates and preserve the value of their international investments.

Establishing a Sustainable System for International Property Management

Managing an international property effectively requires a reliable team, a well-maintained property, and careful financial planning. By selecting a trustworthy local property management company, setting aside funds for maintenance, and actively managing currency exchange considerations, investors can create a sustainable system for overseeing their overseas real estate investments. Consistent communication, regular financial reviews, and proactive maintenance planning ensure that the property remains profitable and attractive to tenants or guests, supporting the long-term success of the investment.

Investors who approach international property management strategically can achieve steady returns and peace of mind, even when operating from afar. Through careful planning and strong partnerships, owning property abroad becomes a manageable, rewarding experience that adds valuable diversification to a real estate portfolio. Whether renting to local tenants or offering short-term stays to global travelers, effective management and financial planning lay the foundation for a successful and resilient international investment.

Chapter 17: Real Estate Development Basics

Understanding the Phases of Real Estate Development

Real estate development is a complex process that transforms raw land or an underutilized property into a valuable asset. The process typically unfolds in distinct phases, each with its own challenges, goals, and requirements. These phases—land acquisition, planning and design, permitting, construction, and marketing—form the backbone of any successful development project. A solid understanding of each phase helps developers navigate the journey from concept to completion, ensuring that each step is executed effectively to meet both financial and project goals.

Land Acquisition and Site Selection

The development process begins with land acquisition and site selection. Choosing the right location is one of the most crucial decisions in real estate development, as location heavily influences market demand, property values, and future profitability. During this phase, developers conduct a detailed site analysis to evaluate factors such as proximity to key amenities, local demographics, zoning regulations, environmental considerations, and infrastructure availability. The goal is to ensure that the chosen site aligns with the intended project and has the potential for appreciation and demand.

In addition to site analysis, feasibility studies play a critical role during land acquisition. A feasibility study examines the project's financial viability by estimating potential revenues, costs, and returns. It helps developers understand whether the proposed development aligns with market demand and provides a realistic return on investment (ROI). Working with market analysts, urban planners, and real estate agents can provide valuable insights, enabling developers to make data-driven decisions on site selection and project scope.

Experienced developer Rachel Morgan shares her insights on site selection: "Location is everything in development. Before I even consider a site, I assess its surroundings, market demand, and any regulatory hurdles. If a site doesn't meet these criteria, I move on. Choosing the right land is the foundation of a successful project." By conducting thorough due diligence during land acquisition, developers set a strong foundation for the rest of the project.

Planning, Design, and Project Approval

Once the site is secured, the planning and design phase begins, transforming the initial vision into a detailed blueprint. During this phase, developers collaborate with architects, engineers, and urban planners to create plans that meet both functional and aesthetic goals. This phase involves extensive design work, covering everything from building layouts and architectural style to landscaping, parking, and utilities. Developers must also ensure that the project meets local zoning requirements, which dictate building height, density, and usage.

Zoning and permitting are essential considerations in this phase. Developers submit project plans to local authorities to obtain necessary permits, which may include land use permits, environmental approvals, and building permits. The permitting process can be complex and time-consuming, often requiring multiple rounds of revisions to meet regulatory standards. Engaging local architects and planners who understand the area's regulations can streamline the process and help avoid costly delays.

In addition to design, this phase includes project budgeting and financing arrangements. A well-structured project budget accounts for all anticipated expenses, such as construction costs, land fees, professional fees, and permits. By creating a comprehensive budget early on, developers can identify funding needs and secure financing before breaking ground. Establishing a clear timeline for each step also helps ensure that the project remains on schedule and within budget.

Architect and project manager Linda Carter explains the importance of this phase: "Planning and design set the stage for everything that follows. The design needs to be both marketable and practical, and permits need to be secured to avoid delays. Good planning is what keeps a project running smoothly from start to finish." By focusing on strategic planning and adhering to regulatory requirements, developers can ensure that their project has a solid foundation and is ready for the next phase.

Construction and Project Management

The construction phase is where the project truly takes shape. This phase involves translating the design plans into a physical structure through skilled construction and careful project management. Developers typically work with general contractors who oversee various trades, such as electricians, plumbers, carpenters, and landscapers. Effective project management is essential to coordinate these teams, manage timelines, and control costs, ensuring that construction progresses according to plan.

Construction timelines can vary depending on project scope, local weather conditions, and material availability. To manage these variables, developers often rely on construction project management software, which helps track progress, schedules, and budgets in real time. Regular site inspections are also crucial to ensure that work is completed according to quality standards and safety regulations.

Developers usually implement contingency plans for potential setbacks, such as delays in material delivery or weather-related issues. Many developers build a contingency fund into the project budget to handle unexpected expenses or overruns. Effective communication between the development team, contractors, and local authorities is also essential to address any issues that arise and keep the project on track.

Project manager and developer Jack Thompson shares his approach to managing construction: "Construction is where a lot of things can go wrong, so keeping everything on schedule and within budget is my top priority. Having a contingency plan and staying flexible helps me manage issues without derailing the entire project." By maintaining control over timelines and costs, developers can ensure a smooth construction process and prepare for the project's final stages.

Marketing, Pre-Leasing, and Project Completion

As construction nears completion, the marketing phase begins. This phase involves promoting the property to potential buyers or tenants, often months before the project is finalized. For residential developments, this may involve creating model units, hosting open houses, or collaborating with real estate agents to generate interest. Commercial developers might focus on securing anchor tenants or pre-leasing retail and office spaces to ensure stable income post-completion.

Effective marketing and pre-leasing strategies can greatly enhance the project's financial success, as they minimize vacancy rates and generate cash flow as soon as the property is ready for occupancy. Developers may use digital marketing, social media, and targeted advertising to reach their target audience, while professional staging and photography can help showcase the property's unique features.

Finally, the project reaches completion, where the property undergoes final inspections and meets all building codes and safety standards. Once approved, the property is handed over to buyers or tenants, marking the official end of the development process. At this point, developers may choose to sell the property to recoup their investment or retain ownership to generate long-term rental income.

Developer Susan Greene shares her insights on project completion: "The last stage is all about showcasing the finished product and making sure every detail is perfect. Marketing and pre-leasing help fill units quickly, so by the time we finish construction, the property is already generating revenue." Successful project completion is the culmination of careful planning, design, and management, transforming the initial vision into a valuable asset.

Building a Foundation for Development Success

Each phase of real estate development plays a crucial role in bringing a project from concept to completion. By understanding and effectively managing each step—land acquisition, planning, construction, and marketing—developers set the stage for a successful project that meets market demand, stays within budget, and generates profitable returns. With a clear approach to each phase, investors and developers can confidently navigate the complexities of development and transform properties into thriving, income-generating assets.

Financing and Budgeting for Development Projects

Financing and budgeting are fundamental to the success of any real estate development project. The ability to secure adequate funding and manage costs effectively throughout the development process can make or break a project. Development financing is more complex than standard real estate loans, as it often requires multiple types of funding, each tailored to a specific phase of the project. From securing construction loans and bridge financing to creating a comprehensive budget that accounts for all anticipated costs, successful developers approach financing and budgeting with meticulous planning and financial discipline.

Exploring Financing Options for Development

Securing the right type of financing is crucial to cover the extensive costs of land acquisition, planning, construction, and marketing. Development projects often require specialized loans that align with the unique stages of the process. One common type of financing for development is the construction loan, a short-term loan designed specifically to fund the building phase. Construction loans are typically structured to release funds in stages, based on the project's progress. For instance, funds may be disbursed upon completing major milestones like site preparation, foundation, framing, and final finishes.

In addition to construction loans, developers may rely on bridge loans to finance the gap between the completion of construction and securing long-term financing or selling the property. Bridge loans are short-term, interest-only loans that provide liquidity during transitional phases. These loans can be essential in cases where a project is ready for occupancy but has not yet generated sufficient income or has not been sold.

Equity partnerships are another financing strategy, where developers bring on investors to share in the project's profits in exchange for funding. Equity partners may be individuals, investment firms, or real estate funds, and their contributions can help cover both initial and ongoing costs. Unlike debt financing, equity financing does not require monthly payments, but it does involve sharing the profits, which can reduce the developer's share of the final returns. For large-scale projects, developers may use a mix of debt and equity financing to optimize their capital structure and reduce financial risk.

Real estate finance consultant James Lee explains the importance of a tailored financing approach: "Every development project is different, so matching the right financing to each stage is essential. Construction loans, bridge loans, and equity partnerships all serve different purposes, and using them strategically allows you to keep cash flowing without over-leveraging." By combining various financing sources, developers can ensure their projects remain financially stable from inception to completion.

Creating a Comprehensive Project Budget

An accurate and detailed budget is essential to managing costs and preventing unexpected financial issues. A development budget typically includes expenses related to land acquisition, construction, permits, professional fees, marketing, and contingencies. Each category should be carefully estimated to ensure the project remains viable, with costs aligned to the project's financial goals.

Land acquisition costs, including purchase price, due diligence fees, and closing costs, are usually one of the first line items in a development budget. Next, construction costs are calculated based on materials, labor, equipment, and subcontractor fees. Because construction can account for a significant portion of the total budget, it's crucial to work closely with contractors and estimators to obtain accurate figures. Estimating each aspect of construction—such as site preparation, foundation, framing, electrical, plumbing, and finishing—ensures that the budget reflects the full scope of work.

In addition to direct costs, developers should allocate funds for professional services, such as architectural design, engineering, legal counsel, and project management. Permits and zoning fees are another important budget component, as these can vary significantly by location and are necessary for compliance. Marketing and sales expenses, including advertising, staging, and real estate commissions, should also be included, especially for residential developments or commercial projects targeting specific tenants.

Contingency funds are essential to account for unexpected expenses, as development projects often encounter unanticipated challenges, such as weather delays, material price increases, or labor shortages. A typical contingency budget ranges from 5% to 15% of the total project cost, depending on the project's complexity and risk factors. By planning for contingencies, developers can handle setbacks without derailing the entire project.

Experienced developer Sarah Blake shares her approach to budgeting: "My budgets are always detailed, down to the last line item. I include a solid contingency, and I regularly review costs as the project progresses. Unexpected expenses can happen, but a well-planned budget helps me stay in control." A thorough, realistic budget provides a roadmap for financial decision-making, helping developers stay on track and avoid cost overruns.

Managing Cash Flow Throughout the Project

Cash flow management is critical in real estate development, as expenses often outpace revenue until the project is completed and sold or leased. Construction and development projects require large cash outflows for land, labor, and materials, but do not generate income until occupancy or sale. As a result, developers must carefully monitor cash flow to ensure they have enough liquidity to cover expenses at each stage.

To manage cash flow effectively, developers often use project milestones as triggers for financing disbursements, particularly when working with construction loans. For example, lenders may release funds incrementally as each phase of construction is completed and inspected. Regular cash flow projections, which estimate cash inflows and outflows over the project timeline, can help developers anticipate funding needs and adjust spending as necessary.

In addition to managing cash flow, developers should carefully monitor their project's loan-to-cost (LTC) ratio, which compares the amount of financing obtained to the total cost of the project. A lower LTC ratio indicates that the developer has put more of their own equity into the project, reducing leverage but potentially improving loan terms. Maintaining a healthy LTC ratio not only improves project stability but also positions the developer for better financing opportunities in future projects.

Property developer Michael Davis emphasizes the importance of cash flow planning: "Cash flow can make or break a project. I monitor it closely, especially during the most capital-intensive stages of construction. A healthy cash flow means I can avoid delays and pay my contractors on time, which keeps the whole project on track." Effective cash flow management allows developers to maintain momentum, reduce financial risk, and complete the project as planned.

Laying the Financial Foundation for Development Success

Financing and budgeting are at the core of successful real estate development, providing the capital and structure needed to bring a project to life. By selecting the right financing options, creating a detailed budget, and managing cash flow, developers can minimize financial risk and keep projects on track. Careful financial planning allows developers to anticipate challenges, respond to changes, and complete their projects within the established timeline and budget, setting the stage for profitable returns.

Through strategic financing and disciplined budgeting, real estate developers can navigate the complexities of development with confidence, laying the groundwork for sustainable growth and successful project outcomes. This solid financial foundation ensures that developers can meet their objectives while managing costs and maximizing their return on investment.

Managing Risks and Maximizing Profitability in Development

Real estate development carries inherent risks, from fluctuating markets to construction delays and unforeseen costs. Successfully managing these risks and strategically planning for profitability are essential for developers who aim to deliver projects on time, within budget, and with a strong return on investment. By understanding potential risks and implementing strategies to mitigate them, developers can enhance project outcomes and increase the likelihood of a profitable venture.

Identifying and Mitigating Development Risks

Development projects are influenced by a variety of external factors that can disrupt timelines, budgets, and profitability. Some of the most common risks include market fluctuations, construction delays, and regulatory changes. Market risk is often tied to economic shifts that affect property demand and pricing. For example, if market conditions weaken during a project's timeline, the expected sales or rental rates could decrease, reducing anticipated returns. To mitigate market risk, developers often conduct comprehensive market research and feasibility studies to ensure there's a demand for the project and to forecast potential profitability.

Construction delays are another frequent challenge in real estate development, often caused by weather, labor shortages, or material delays. These setbacks can lead to increased costs and extended timelines, ultimately impacting profitability. Developers can minimize the impact of construction delays by selecting reliable contractors, setting realistic timelines, and maintaining a well-organized project management process. Many developers also establish relationships with multiple suppliers to secure backup sources for key materials and avoid delays from supplier shortages.

Regulatory and permitting risks can also disrupt a project. Unexpected changes in zoning laws, building codes, or environmental regulations may require costly adjustments to plans. Working with local consultants and legal advisors during the planning stage helps developers understand and comply with relevant regulations, reducing the likelihood of regulatory obstacles. Building contingencies into the project plan also provides a safety net, allowing developers to adapt without jeopardizing the project's overall feasibility.

Developer Sarah Lindstrom explains her approach to risk management: "Every project has risks, but being proactive is key. I always have backup plans for suppliers and maintain a close relationship with local authorities to stay updated on regulatory changes. Planning for these issues upfront means fewer surprises during development." By identifying and planning for risks early on, developers can navigate challenges more effectively, ensuring the project progresses smoothly.

Implementing Strategies for Cost Control and Profit Maximization

Controlling costs is fundamental to profitability in real estate development, and developers employ several strategies to manage expenses and enhance profit margins. One effective strategy is negotiating fixed-price contracts with contractors, where the agreed price covers all labor and materials for a specific scope of work. Fixed-price contracts limit the risk of unexpected cost increases, allowing developers to maintain tighter control over the budget. Alternatively, if using a cost-plus contract (where the developer pays for materials and labor plus a contractor markup), developers should establish a maximum cost threshold to prevent budget overruns.

Value engineering is another powerful tool for maximizing profitability. Value engineering involves analyzing the project design to find cost-saving opportunities without compromising quality or functionality. For example, selecting durable yet affordable materials, optimizing the layout to reduce unnecessary space, or using energy-efficient systems can all reduce costs while adding value to the final product. Developers often work closely with architects and engineers to identify these adjustments, ensuring the project remains appealing and marketable.

Monitoring project timelines also plays a crucial role in profitability, as delays can increase carrying costs, such as interest on loans and property taxes. Developers who consistently meet project milestones avoid these added expenses and are able to bring the property to market faster, allowing them to capitalize on favorable market conditions. A detailed project schedule, regular progress tracking, and contingency plans for potential delays all contribute to maintaining project timelines.

Cost manager and developer Jack Moreno shares his cost-control approach: "I believe in meticulous planning and regular budget reviews. I work with my team to identify cost-saving options and monitor our timeline closely. Every saved dollar goes directly to the bottom line, which makes a big difference in the end." Effective cost management and timeline control enable developers to protect their budget and maximize potential returns.

Choosing Locations and Project Designs for Higher Profitability

Strategic location selection and market-responsive design are two factors that significantly impact a development project's profitability. Properties in high-growth areas with strong demand—such as urban centers, emerging neighborhoods, or popular suburban regions—tend to attract higher sale prices or rental rates, resulting in increased returns. Developers should assess local market trends, population growth, and economic indicators when choosing a project location, as these factors influence both demand and appreciation potential.

Creating a market-responsive design ensures that the development meets the specific needs and preferences of the target audience. For example, a residential development in a family-oriented suburb may benefit from offering spacious layouts, multiple bedrooms, and child-friendly amenities. Conversely, a project in a vibrant urban area might focus on compact units with modern finishes and shared spaces for socializing, catering to young professionals. Understanding and catering to the preferences of the intended market not only enhances the appeal of the property but also allows for premium pricing.

Developers may also incorporate eco-friendly features and sustainable design elements, which are increasingly popular and can set the project apart in a competitive market. Features like energy-efficient appliances, green roofs, and sustainable building materials appeal to environmentally conscious buyers and renters, potentially commanding higher prices or rental rates. Green certifications, such as LEED (Leadership in Energy and Environmental Design), can also add value, positioning the project as a premium offering.

Developer and project strategist Emily Zhang highlights the importance of aligning design with market demand: "Every project I work on is tailored to the local market. I study what buyers and renters are looking for and design accordingly. By offering exactly what the market wants, I'm able to maximize profitability and minimize vacancy rates." Designing with the end user in mind ensures that the property meets demand, increasing its appeal and profitability potential.

Achieving Success through Risk Management and Strategic Profit Planning

Managing risks and enhancing profitability are key objectives in real estate development, requiring a combination of careful planning, cost control, and market insight. By identifying potential risks early, controlling costs through efficient contracts and value engineering, and choosing high-demand locations with market-responsive designs, developers can complete projects that not only meet their financial goals but also add value to the community.

Real estate development is inherently challenging, but those who approach each project with a strategic mindset and a proactive approach to risk management can achieve profitable, sustainable outcomes. By building these principles into every stage of development, developers can consistently deliver projects that succeed in dynamic markets, transforming challenges into opportunities and laying the groundwork for long-term success.

Chapter 18: Sustainable and Green Building Practic

Key Principles of Sustainable Building Design

Sustainable building design centers around creating structures that reduce environmental impact, promote resource efficiency, and provide healthier living or working spaces. The core principles of sustainable building—energy efficiency, resource conservation, and the use of eco-friendly materials—form the foundation for developing properties that not only meet the needs of occupants but also support environmental stewardship. These principles help developers create buildings with lower operating costs, reduced resource demands, and increased long-term value.

Energy Efficiency and Renewable Energy Integration

Energy efficiency is a primary focus in sustainable building design, as reducing energy consumption directly benefits both the environment and the property's operating costs. Energy-efficient buildings minimize the use of non-renewable resources, lower greenhouse gas emissions, and decrease utility expenses. Effective strategies include improving insulation, sealing windows and doors, and using energy-efficient appliances and lighting. For example, LED lighting consumes significantly less electricity than traditional bulbs, lowering energy use and reducing maintenance needs due to their longer lifespan.

Integrating renewable energy sources, such as solar panels or wind turbines, can further enhance a building's sustainability. Solar panels are particularly popular for residential and commercial properties, as they convert sunlight into electricity, which can offset or even eliminate dependency on the grid. Many government programs offer tax credits or rebates to incentivize solar energy adoption, making it a cost-effective choice in the long term. Properties equipped with renewable energy systems not only reduce their carbon footprint but can also achieve net-zero energy consumption, where the building generates as much energy as it uses.

Architect and sustainability expert Lisa Carrington explains, "The key to a truly energy-efficient building is layering different strategies. Combining strong insulation with smart energy use and renewable energy sources results in a property that's both cost-effective and environmentally friendly." By focusing on energy efficiency and renewable energy integration, developers can create buildings that align with modern sustainability goals and offer long-term economic benefits.

Maximizing Natural Light and Ventilation

Another core principle of sustainable building design is maximizing natural light and ventilation, which enhances occupant comfort while reducing energy costs. Strategic placement of windows, skylights, and glass doors allows natural light to flood interior spaces, minimizing the need for artificial lighting during the day. Natural light not only reduces energy consumption but also has been shown to improve mood and productivity, making it a valuable feature for both residential and commercial buildings.

Ventilation is equally important for maintaining indoor air quality and regulating temperature naturally. Well-designed ventilation systems enable fresh air to circulate, reducing reliance on heating, ventilation, and air conditioning (HVAC) systems and improving the indoor environment. Passive ventilation techniques, such as operable windows and air vents, allow air to flow naturally through the building, while energy-efficient HVAC systems can be used to supplement ventilation as needed. Green roofs and vertical gardens are additional features that help regulate temperature, improving both insulation and air quality.

Developer John Dawson highlights the value of natural light and ventilation: "When I design properties, I focus on bringing the outside in. Natural light and ventilation lower energy costs and create a space that feels open and connected to the environment." Embracing natural light and airflow in building design not only enhances sustainability but also creates healthier, more enjoyable spaces for occupants.

Water Conservation and Sustainable Landscaping

Water conservation is another critical element of sustainable building design, especially in regions prone to droughts or water scarcity. Buildings that conserve water reduce demand on local water supplies and lower utility costs. Common strategies for water conservation include installing low-flow fixtures, dual-flush toilets, and water-efficient appliances. For example, low-flow showerheads and faucets limit water usage without sacrificing performance, leading to substantial savings over time.

Sustainable landscaping is also an important consideration, as it reduces water consumption and supports local ecosystems.

Native plants, which are adapted to the local climate, require less water, fertilizer, and maintenance, making them ideal for sustainable landscapes. Rain gardens and permeable paving are additional options for managing stormwater, as they allow rainwater to filter into the ground, reducing runoff and replenishing groundwater supplies.

Landscaping expert Sarah Thompson emphasizes the importance of sustainable practices: "Choosing native plants and water-smart landscaping not only conserves resources but creates beautiful, low-maintenance green spaces that are in harmony with the local environment." By incorporating water conservation practices and sustainable landscaping, developers can create environmentally responsible properties that contribute to local biodiversity and reduce water waste.

Creating Sustainable and Resilient Properties

Adopting the core principles of sustainable building design—energy efficiency, natural light and ventilation, and water conservation—helps developers create properties that are both eco-friendly and resilient. These sustainable design choices benefit the environment, reduce operating costs, and contribute to healthier, more comfortable spaces for occupants. As sustainability becomes increasingly valued by both regulators and consumers, buildings that embody these principles are more likely to retain value, attract tenants or buyers, and provide long-term returns.

By focusing on these foundational elements, developers and investors can meet current demands for sustainability while future-proofing their properties in an evolving real estate market. Sustainable building design not only supports environmental goals but also aligns with the growing expectation for properties that are resource-efficient, cost-effective, and environmentally responsible.

Selecting Eco-Friendly Materials and Technologies

Choosing eco-friendly materials and incorporating sustainable technologies are crucial steps in green building practices. By prioritizing environmentally responsible materials and advanced technologies, developers can reduce a property's environmental impact, improve energy efficiency, and enhance indoor air quality. Selecting sustainable materials and energy-efficient systems not only benefits the environment but also appeals to eco-conscious buyers and tenants, making the property more attractive in a competitive market.

Choosing Sustainable and Recycled Materials

Sustainable materials play a key role in green building, as they reduce the environmental impact associated with sourcing, manufacturing, and disposal. Many eco-friendly materials are made from renewable resources, are recyclable, or have a low carbon footprint. For example, bamboo and cork are rapidly renewable and versatile materials that can be used for flooring, cabinetry, and wall coverings. These materials grow quickly, regenerate without extensive replanting, and require minimal pesticides or fertilizers, making them eco-friendly alternatives to hardwood.

Recycled materials, such as reclaimed wood, recycled metal, and concrete made with recycled aggregates, also help lower environmental impact. Reclaimed wood, for example, offers unique textures and aesthetics, giving spaces character while reducing the need for new lumber. Likewise, recycled metal and concrete decrease the demand for virgin materials, lowering greenhouse gas emissions associated with mining and production.

Architect and sustainability advocate Lisa Thompson explains the value of sustainable materials: "I always try to source materials that are renewable, recycled, or have a lower environmental footprint. Not only does it reduce waste, but it also creates a unique look and feel that resonates with clients." By selecting materials that have minimal environmental impact, developers can create buildings that are both beautiful and sustainable.

Implementing Energy-Efficient Technologies

In addition to sustainable materials, energy-efficient technologies significantly contribute to green building practices by reducing energy consumption and lowering operating costs. Modern HVAC systems, for instance, are designed to use energy more efficiently, providing consistent heating and cooling while minimizing energy waste. Heat recovery ventilation (HRV) systems are particularly beneficial, as they capture heat from exhausted air and use it to warm incoming fresh air, reducing the demand on heating systems.

Smart thermostats are another popular energy-efficient technology, allowing users to control heating and cooling remotely and set schedules that optimize energy use. Smart thermostats monitor occupancy and adjust temperatures automatically, preventing energy waste when spaces are unoccupied. This technology is especially useful in multi-unit buildings, where centralized energy management can lead to significant savings and reduce a building's overall carbon footprint.

Lighting systems are also essential for energy efficiency. LED lighting uses up to 80% less energy than traditional incandescent bulbs and has a much longer lifespan, reducing maintenance and replacement costs. Many developers now incorporate daylight sensors and occupancy sensors, which automatically adjust lighting based on natural light availability and room occupancy. By investing in advanced lighting technologies, developers can reduce electricity usage and enhance energy efficiency.

Energy consultant Mark Ruiz emphasizes the importance of energy-efficient systems: "Choosing energy-efficient HVAC and lighting systems is one of the most effective ways to reduce a building's operational costs. These technologies pay off in the long run and make the property more sustainable overall." Incorporating energy-efficient systems into building design not only lowers energy bills but also reduces the environmental impact associated with energy production.

Integrating Water-Saving Fixtures and Smart Home Technologies

Water-saving fixtures and smart home technologies further enhance the sustainability of a building by reducing water consumption and enabling more efficient resource management. Low-flow fixtures, such as faucets, showerheads, and toilets, use less water without sacrificing performance. Dual-flush toilets offer users the option to choose between a low and high water flow, conserving water by reducing usage for liquid waste. These fixtures can lead to substantial water savings, especially in multi-unit residential buildings.

Smart home technologies provide enhanced control over a building's energy and water usage. For example, smart irrigation systems automatically adjust water levels based on weather conditions, preventing overwatering and conserving water in landscaping. Similarly, smart home energy monitors track power consumption in real time, helping occupants and property managers identify high-use areas and adjust their habits to save energy.

Other smart home devices, such as smart plugs and energy monitors, give property managers and residents more control over energy consumption. For instance, smart plugs can be programmed to shut off appliances during off-peak hours, or when they are not in use, reducing unnecessary electricity consumption. These systems create a more responsive, energy-efficient environment, allowing buildings to operate at peak efficiency while minimizing resource use.

Property manager Rachel Lee highlights the benefits of smart technology: "By integrating smart systems for water and energy use, we've reduced our overall consumption significantly. These technologies not only help us save money but also meet the expectations of eco-conscious tenants." Smart technology not only improves sustainability but also offers modern conveniences that appeal to today's tenants, adding value and competitiveness to the property.

Building Sustainable and Cost-Efficient Properties with Technology and Materials

The careful selection of eco-friendly materials and energy-efficient technologies is essential for creating sustainable buildings that meet today's environmental standards and market demands. By prioritizing materials that are renewable, recycled, or locally sourced, developers can reduce a property's carbon footprint and contribute to more responsible resource use. At the same time, incorporating energy-efficient systems and smart home technologies enhances operational efficiency, conserves resources, and provides cost savings for property owners and tenants.

Integrating these elements into building design results in a more sustainable property that aligns with evolving environmental priorities and appeals to a growing demographic of eco-conscious occupants. Through thoughtful choices in materials and technology, developers can create buildings that stand the test of time, offer lower operating costs, and make a positive impact on the environment. Sustainable practices not only enhance the property's performance but also position it as a forward-thinking, responsible investment in an increasingly green-focused market.

Implementing Green Building Certifications and Standards

Green building certifications, such as LEED, WELL, and BREEAM, provide structured frameworks for sustainable design, construction, and operation. Achieving certification not only demonstrates a commitment to environmental responsibility but also enhances a property's appeal, value, and marketability. Certified buildings often enjoy advantages such as tax incentives, energy savings, and higher occupancy rates, as they align with the growing demand for eco-friendly spaces. Understanding these certifications and implementing their standards can help developers achieve both environmental and financial goals, creating properties that are recognized for their sustainability.

LEED Certification: Leadership in Energy and Environmental Design

LEED (Leadership in Energy and Environmental Design), developed by the U.S. Green Building Council, is one of the most widely recognized green building certification systems globally. LEED provides a comprehensive framework covering energy use, water efficiency, materials selection, indoor environmental quality, and sustainable site development. Buildings earn points across these categories to achieve certification levels, ranging from LEED Certified to LEED Platinum, with higher levels signifying stronger sustainability performance.

LEED certification requires developers to consider sustainability at every stage of development, from site selection and design to construction and maintenance. For example, to earn points in the energy category, developers might implement high-efficiency HVAC systems, LED lighting, or renewable energy sources like solar panels. To address water efficiency, they might install low-flow fixtures and water-efficient landscaping. Indoor air quality is also prioritized, with points awarded for proper ventilation, the use of low-VOC (volatile organic compound) materials, and access to natural light.

Real estate developer Hannah Green shares her experience with LEED: "The LEED framework guides us to build more responsibly, ensuring that we're not only meeting market expectations but actually creating healthier environments. It's challenging but rewarding to see the certification come together and know we're making a difference." LEED certification not only helps reduce environmental impact but also increases a property's appeal to environmentally conscious tenants and buyers.

WELL Certification: Prioritizing Health and Wellbeing

While LEED emphasizes environmental performance, WELL certification, developed by the International WELL Building Institute, focuses on human health and wellbeing within the built environment. WELL examines how a building impacts its occupants' physical and mental health, covering aspects like air quality, lighting, water quality, nourishment, and community connection. The certification is designed to create spaces that promote healthier lifestyles and enhance the overall experience of occupants.

WELL certification requires rigorous attention to details that impact health, such as ensuring optimal air filtration, providing access to filtered drinking water, using lighting systems that support circadian rhythms, and even incorporating design elements that encourage physical movement, such as stair accessibility and fitness amenities. For example, buildings may earn points for providing indoor air quality that exceeds industry standards, minimizing exposure to indoor pollutants, and offering adequate natural light to reduce eye strain and improve mood.

Tenant feedback on WELL-certified spaces has been overwhelmingly positive, as people increasingly prioritize wellness in their living and working environments. Property manager Lisa

Cheng emphasizes the value of WELL certification: "The WELL standards help us create spaces where people feel comfortable, energized, and safe. It's more than a certification—it's about creating spaces that positively impact daily life." With WELL certification, developers not only contribute to occupant wellbeing but also improve tenant retention and satisfaction, resulting in a highly desirable property.

BREEAM Certification: A Comprehensive International Standard

BREEAM (Building Research Establishment Environmental Assessment Method) is one of the oldest and most established green building certification systems, originating in the UK and widely used in Europe and beyond. BREEAM provides a holistic approach to assessing building sustainability, covering management, energy, health, water, materials, waste, and land use. Like LEED, BREEAM awards certification at different levels (Pass, Good, Very Good, Excellent, and Outstanding), based on a points system.

BREEAM's strength lies in its flexibility and adaptability to various types of buildings, from commercial offices to multi-family residences and industrial facilities. The system encourages developers to go beyond regulatory standards, rewarding them for innovation and long-term sustainability planning. For example, BREEAM-certified buildings often feature rainwater harvesting systems, green roofs, and advanced waste management solutions. In addition, BREEAM places a strong emphasis on responsible sourcing of materials, ensuring that developers choose suppliers that adhere to sustainable practices.

Green building consultant David Lin highlights the importance of BREEAM: "BREEAM is internationally recognized, making it a great choice for developers working globally. Its comprehensive scope pushes projects to think long-term and implement practices that reduce environmental impact across all areas." BREEAM certification not only provides environmental benefits but also offers a valuable selling point, particularly for international investors and tenants who prioritize sustainability.

Achieving Certification and Adding Value through Sustainable Standards

Implementing green building certifications and standards enhances a property's environmental and market value. While each certification has its own focus—LEED on environmental impact, WELL on human health, and BREEAM on comprehensive sustainability—each one brings substantial benefits to both developers and occupants. Certified buildings appeal to a growing segment of environmentally conscious tenants and buyers, enjoy higher occupancy rates, and often qualify for incentives or rebates from local governments.

Developers interested in certification should engage with accredited professionals early in the design process to ensure compliance with the chosen standard. Achieving certification requires careful planning, documentation, and adherence to best practices throughout the project. However, the long-term benefits, from reduced operating costs to increased tenant satisfaction, make certification a sound investment in sustainability.

By committing to green building certifications, developers not only contribute positively to the environment but also create more resilient, valuable properties that meet the expectations of modern occupants. Green certifications position a property as a forward-thinking, high-quality investment, enhancing its long-term appeal and profitability in a marketplace that increasingly values sustainability. Through LEED, WELL, BREEAM, or other green standards, developers can make a lasting impact on the environment and the communities they serve, while benefiting from enhanced market positioning and financial returns.

Chapter 19: Navigating Market Downturns

Preparing for Market Downturns with a Strong Financial Foundation

A solid financial foundation is essential for real estate investors to weather market downturns and avoid making hasty, loss-inducing decisions. Building financial resilience before a downturn strikes allows investors to hold onto properties without pressure to sell at a discount, maintain cash flow even during tough times, and emerge from downturns in a position to capitalize on new opportunities. Key components of a strong financial foundation include maintaining adequate cash reserves, managing debt conservatively, and prioritizing cash flow stability.

Building an Emergency Cash Reserve

One of the most effective ways to prepare for a market downturn is by maintaining a cash reserve—funds set aside specifically for unexpected expenses or periods of reduced income. Cash reserves act as a buffer, allowing investors to cover operating expenses, property maintenance, and mortgage payments during times of reduced rental income or increased vacancy. By having these funds readily available, investors can avoid the need to liquidate properties at unfavorable prices simply to cover short-term costs.

The ideal size of a cash reserve depends on several factors, including the size of the portfolio, the stability of rental income, and the market's volatility. For many investors, a reserve that covers six to twelve months of operating expenses and debt payments is recommended. Investors with larger portfolios or properties in highly cyclical markets may choose to maintain a more substantial reserve. In addition to covering property expenses, a cash reserve can also serve as a cushion for personal financial needs, reducing the likelihood that an investor's own income challenges affect their ability to manage the portfolio.

Financial advisor David Kim emphasizes the importance of a cash reserve: "Having cash on hand during a downturn can make all the difference. It allows you to stay in control, make calculated decisions, and hold onto properties until the market improves. Without that cushion, you're at the mercy of the market." By building and maintaining an emergency reserve, investors can withstand temporary setbacks without compromising long-term investment goals.

Managing Debt with a Conservative Approach

Debt management is another critical factor in preparing for market downturns. During periods of economic growth, it can be tempting to take on additional leverage to expand a portfolio rapidly. However, in a declining market, high debt levels can become a liability, as lower rental income and higher vacancies make it challenging to meet debt obligations. Maintaining a conservative loan-to-value (LTV) ratio—such as 60% to 70% rather than 80% or higher—reduces the risk of financial strain in a downturn and provides greater flexibility.

Choosing fixed-rate loans over variable-rate loans can also mitigate risk. Fixed-rate loans lock in interest rates, ensuring predictable monthly payments, even if interest rates rise in response to economic changes. This stability can be invaluable during downturns, as variable-rate loans may become increasingly expensive to service when the economy is unstable. Additionally, avoiding short-term, high-interest debt helps investors manage cash flow more effectively, as longer-term loans typically offer lower monthly payments and provide more time for the market to recover.

Real estate investor Laura Brooks shares her debt management strategy: "I focus on keeping my LTV ratio conservative and only use fixed-rate loans. This way, my debt payments stay predictable, and I'm not over-leveraged if rental income dips. It's about building a portfolio that can withstand both good and bad times." By approaching debt conservatively, investors can reduce financial pressure and retain control of their properties, even during challenging economic periods.

Prioritizing Cash Flow Stability Over Short-Term Appreciation

While property appreciation is often a desirable goal, cash flow stability should take precedence when preparing for a downturn. Properties with positive, reliable cash flow provide a steady income that can help investors cover expenses and stay solvent during market declines. Properties that generate consistent cash flow are particularly valuable during downturns, as they reduce dependency on property sales for profit and provide the income needed to ride out tough times.

When selecting properties, investors should focus on areas and property types with strong rental demand, even during economic slowdowns. Affordable housing, multifamily properties, and properties located near essential services or major employment centers often perform well during downturns, as they attract tenants who are less likely to vacate due to economic conditions. Additionally, long-term leases with stable tenants, such as commercial properties leased to essential businesses, can provide security and predictable income in volatile markets.

Investors who prioritize cash flow stability over speculative appreciation are better positioned to maintain their portfolios during downturns. Financial planner Eric Martinez advises, "A property that generates steady income is invaluable in a downturn. Even if property values fall temporarily, that cash flow helps you keep the lights on, pay down debt, and avoid forced sales." By focusing on properties with stable cash flow, investors can sustain themselves through market lows without sacrificing their long-term investment potential.

Building a Resilient Financial Foundation for Long-Term Success

Preparing for market downturns requires more than just optimism—it demands a resilient financial strategy that safeguards against the unpredictable. By maintaining a cash reserve, managing debt conservatively, and prioritizing cash flow stability, investors build a solid foundation that enables them to endure market fluctuations and avoid the pressure to make hasty decisions. A robust financial foundation not only enhances an investor's ability to withstand downturns but also positions them to seize new opportunities when the market recovers.

In real estate, resilience is built over time through thoughtful financial planning and disciplined decision-making. By focusing on financial preparedness, investors can navigate downturns with confidence and emerge from challenging periods with their portfolios intact, ready to capitalize on future growth opportunities.

Adapting Investment Strategies During Economic Downturns

In an economic downturn, flexible and adaptive investment strategies become crucial. While high-growth assets may be enticing in a booming market, a more resilient approach is necessary when the market declines. During these times, successful investors focus on value-add opportunities, shift their attention to recession-resistant property types, and adjust their portfolio priorities to minimize risk and maximize stability. By recalibrating strategies to match current market conditions, investors can maintain profitability and safeguard their portfolios.

Focusing on Value-Add Opportunities

Value-add properties, which allow investors to increase a property's worth through improvements, offer significant advantages during downturns. In a declining market, properties with untapped potential can be transformed to attract higher rents or sell at a premium, even when the broader market is experiencing a slowdown. Common value-add strategies include renovating interiors, updating building systems (such as HVAC or plumbing), enhancing curb appeal, or adding amenities like laundry facilities or community spaces.

Investors can find value-add opportunities in both residential and commercial properties, targeting properties that are underperforming or in need of updates. For example, a poorly maintained apartment building in a desirable location can become more attractive to tenants after strategic upgrades, leading to higher occupancy rates and rental income. Value-add investments provide investors with the flexibility to create value independent of market conditions, allowing them to improve cash flow and property value through operational and physical improvements rather than relying solely on market appreciation.

Real estate investor and property manager Alicia Torres shares her approach to value-add investing: "In a downturn, I look for properties where I can make improvements that tenants will pay for—upgraded units, better amenities, or even energy-efficient appliances. These upgrades make my properties more appealing and help maintain rent levels, even if the market is down." By focusing on value-add strategies, investors can increase income potential and property value, providing a buffer against market declines.

Exploring Recession-Resistant Property Types

Some property types are more resilient to economic downturns than others, as they cater to stable demand regardless of broader economic conditions. Affordable housing, essential retail spaces, and multifamily properties often perform better during recessions, as they address fundamental needs that people continue to prioritize, even in tough times. Shifting focus to these recession-resistant properties can help investors maintain occupancy rates and income stability during market downturns.

Affordable housing, for instance, typically experiences consistent demand, as it caters to individuals and families with limited budgets. Multifamily properties also offer stability by diversifying rental income across multiple units, reducing the impact of any single vacancy. For commercial investors, properties leased to essential businesses—such as grocery stores, pharmacies, and healthcare facilities—are less likely to face closures during economic slowdowns, offering reliable income.

Investor Marcus Reid explains his approach to targeting recession-resistant properties: "When the market's uncertain, I focus on assets that cater to basic needs. Affordable housing and essential retail are usually safe bets, as people always need places to live and shop for essentials. These investments help me keep my portfolio steady." By prioritizing property types that are less vulnerable to economic fluctuations, investors can enhance portfolio stability and reduce exposure to high-risk assets.

Adjusting Portfolio Priorities for Risk Mitigation

During a downturn, investors may need to reassess their portfolio priorities, shifting focus from growth to stability. This often involves holding or repositioning assets, reducing high-risk investments, and concentrating on properties with reliable income streams. For example, investors holding speculative properties in volatile markets may consider selling or re-evaluating these assets to reduce exposure. Instead, they may prioritize core properties in stable locations with proven demand.

Repositioning assets within a portfolio can also mean changing property use or lease terms to better match market demand. For instance, a commercial property that previously catered to discretionary retail could be re-leased to essential services or converted to accommodate multiple tenants. Investors might also consider renegotiating lease terms to secure long-term tenants, locking in predictable cash flow for a specified period. Adapting lease structures and tenancy arrangements can increase income stability and mitigate the risk of vacancies.

Investment advisor Sarah Blake emphasizes the importance of shifting priorities in a downturn: "When the market slows, my clients and I focus on income stability over appreciation. We look at how each asset contributes to cash flow and make adjustments to ensure the portfolio can handle any further declines. It's all about staying flexible and thinking long-term." By adjusting portfolio priorities, investors can enhance resilience, focusing on assets that generate steady returns and reducing the impact of fluctuating market values.

Building a Flexible and Resilient Investment Strategy

Adapting investment strategies during economic downturns requires flexibility, resilience, and a focus on assets that continue to perform despite market challenges. By prioritizing value-add opportunities, targeting recession-resistant properties, and re-evaluating portfolio priorities, investors can navigate downturns with greater confidence and stability. This proactive approach not only protects existing assets but also positions investors to capitalize on profitable opportunities as market conditions improve.

A flexible investment strategy that responds to changing economic conditions allows investors to make the most of downturns, maximizing resilience and preparing for eventual market recovery. By recalibrating their approach to align with current challenges, real estate investors can maintain cash flow, protect portfolio value, and continue building long-term wealth.

Leveraging Opportunities and Positioning for Recovery

While market downturns pose challenges, they also create unique opportunities for real estate investors who are prepared to act strategically. Those with liquidity, a long-term perspective, and a readiness to make calculated investments can often acquire valuable assets at discounted prices, positioning their portfolios for substantial gains when the market rebounds. By identifying undervalued properties, negotiating favorable purchase terms, and planning for recovery, investors can transform economic downturns into periods of growth and set themselves up for success in the next cycle.

Identifying Undervalued Properties and Distressed Assets

During downturns, some property owners face financial strain and may need to sell assets quickly, creating opportunities for buyers to acquire properties at lower-than-market prices. Distressed properties—those that are financially underperforming or in need of improvements—often come with a discount, as sellers prioritize quick sales over maximizing price. For investors, purchasing these assets provides a chance to buy low and benefit from potential appreciation and improved cash flow as the market recovers.

In a downturn, properties in good locations but facing temporary financial challenges can offer excellent investment potential. Investors can add value to these assets through renovations, operational improvements, or better management practices, ultimately increasing their worth. Properties in prime areas, such as city centers or high-demand neighborhoods, tend to recover quickly, allowing investors to achieve higher occupancy rates and rental income once the market stabilizes.

Real estate investor Dan Monroe shares his approach to identifying undervalued assets: "In a downturn, I look for properties in strong locations that may be struggling temporarily. These properties often need minor updates or better management to bring them back up to their true value. It's a great way to buy quality assets at a discount." By targeting properties with strong fundamentals but temporary challenges, investors can capitalize on downturns to expand their portfolios with high-quality assets.

Negotiating Favorable Purchase Terms

Downturns create a buyer's market, providing investors with greater leverage to negotiate favorable purchase terms. With fewer buyers in the market, sellers are often more willing to accept flexible financing arrangements, lower purchase prices, or concessions on closing costs. Buyers may also negotiate for contingencies that allow them to back out or re-negotiate if financing changes or property inspections reveal unexpected issues. For investors, these favorable terms not only reduce upfront costs but also provide flexibility and protection in an uncertain market.

In addition to price reductions, seller financing can become a viable option during downturns. Seller financing allows buyers to pay the seller in installments rather than securing a traditional loan, which can be beneficial if bank financing is difficult to obtain. Seller-financed deals are often more flexible and can include terms like lower interest rates, extended repayment periods, or even balloon payments. This structure reduces the buyer's immediate financial burden and can help stabilize cash flow, allowing for more strategic financial planning.

Investment advisor Sara Blake highlights the benefits of negotiating in a down market: "A downturn is the perfect time to negotiate, whether it's on price, financing, or closing terms. Sellers are more open to deals that would be difficult in a stronger market, so there's room to secure terms that reduce risk and improve cash flow." By capitalizing on a buyer's market, investors can secure better deals, positioning themselves for profitability even before the market fully recovers.

Positioning for Long-Term Appreciation and Market Recovery

While downturns can be unsettling, they are also temporary, and history has shown that real estate markets recover and appreciate over time. Investors with a long-term perspective can use downturns to acquire assets that are likely to grow in value as the market rebounds. By holding onto properties through the downturn and maintaining them well, investors can enjoy significant gains when demand returns. Additionally, properties purchased at a discount can be refinanced as the market improves, allowing investors to pull equity out for further investment or capitalize on lower interest rates.

Investors can further enhance their portfolio's recovery potential by making strategic improvements during the downturn, positioning properties to attract tenants or buyers once demand increases. Renovations, modernized amenities, or energy-efficient upgrades can make properties more appealing, increasing rental income and property value. Properties that are well-maintained and updated are often among the first to attract tenants or buyers in a recovering market, giving investors an edge when occupancy and demand pick up.

Investor and property manager James Connors shares his long-term strategy: "In a downturn, I don't just sit back—I prepare my properties to be top contenders when the market improves. By investing in upgrades and positioning them well, I know they'll perform strongly when demand returns. It's about thinking long-term and making sure my portfolio is ready to benefit from recovery." By proactively positioning assets for appreciation, investors can make the most of a rebounding market and achieve higher returns.

Capitalizing on Downturns for Strategic Growth

Market downturns can be difficult, but they also provide valuable opportunities for investors who take a proactive, long-term approach. By identifying undervalued assets, negotiating favorable terms, and positioning properties for recovery, investors can build a resilient portfolio poised for future success. This approach allows investors to not only survive downturns but also leverage them for strategic growth, creating a competitive advantage as the market stabilizes.

The real estate market's cyclical nature means that downturns are inevitable, but by viewing these periods as opportunities rather than obstacles, investors can emerge stronger and better prepared for future growth. A focus on strategic acquisition, favorable financing, and long-term planning transforms downturns into periods of expansion, setting the stage for sustainable success in the years to come.

Chapter 20: Scaling a Real Estate Business

Building a Strong Foundation with Systems and Processes

Scaling a real estate business requires more than just acquiring additional properties; it demands streamlined systems and processes that support growth without overwhelming the investor. By establishing a strong operational foundation, investors can handle the complexities of a larger portfolio, reduce manual tasks, and ensure that each property is managed consistently and efficiently. Effective systems in areas like property management, accounting, lead generation, and deal analysis are the backbone of a scalable real estate business, providing the stability and efficiency needed to grow with confidence.

Setting Up Core Systems for Property Management and Maintenance

A scalable real estate business relies on efficient property management systems that streamline day-to-day operations, from tenant communication to maintenance requests. Property management software, such as Buildium, AppFolio, or Rent Manager, can centralize tasks like rent collection, lease management, and tenant screening, allowing investors to handle multiple properties without being overwhelmed by administrative work. By automating these functions, investors ensure that rental payments are tracked, leases are organized, and tenant interactions are recorded, reducing the risk of errors and freeing up time for other strategic activities.

A structured approach to property maintenance is also essential for scalability. Developing a maintenance protocol—such as regular inspections, preventive maintenance schedules, and standardized processes for handling repairs—helps prevent small issues from escalating into costly problems. Many investors use maintenance management software to track work orders, communicate with contractors, and document repairs. Additionally, creating a list of reliable local contractors ensures quick responses to maintenance needs, providing tenants with a better experience and preserving property value.

Property investor Sarah Nelson shares her experience with management systems: "When I first started, I handled everything manually, but as my portfolio grew, it became impossible. Implementing property management software saved me countless hours and improved my tenant relationships. Everything is tracked and organized, making it easy to manage multiple properties without missing a beat." By setting up effective property management systems, investors can scale confidently, knowing that their properties are well-maintained and tenant interactions are seamless.

Streamlining Accounting and Financial Management

A robust accounting system is essential for tracking income, expenses, taxes, and overall portfolio performance as a real estate business grows. Manually managing finances for a handful of properties might be manageable, but as the portfolio expands, an automated accounting solution becomes necessary.

Software like QuickBooks, Stessa, or REI Hub allows investors to track rental income, categorize expenses, and generate financial reports. By keeping accurate records, investors can identify profit and loss trends, assess property performance, and prepare for tax season without scrambling to gather receipts and statements.

Beyond software, developing standardized processes for financial management, such as setting up dedicated bank accounts for each property or organizing monthly cash flow reviews, can improve transparency and accountability. Regular financial audits allow investors to monitor expenses and ensure each property meets its cash flow targets. With well-organized accounting, investors can make informed decisions based on real-time financial insights, which is especially valuable when deciding whether to hold, sell, or reinvest in a property.

CPA and real estate advisor Michael Turner emphasizes the importance of financial systems: "Having organized, accessible financial records is crucial as your business grows. It helps you identify profitable properties, understand tax obligations, and make better investment decisions. Good accounting practices set you up for long-term success." By implementing comprehensive accounting systems, investors gain financial clarity, enabling them to manage a growing portfolio effectively.

Automating Lead Generation and Deal Analysis

To scale a real estate business, consistent deal flow and efficient analysis are essential. Establishing an automated lead generation process helps investors identify and evaluate new opportunities without spending excessive time searching for deals. Online platforms like Zillow, Redfin, and LoopNet can be used to set up alerts for specific property types, locations, and price ranges. Additionally, tools like DealCheck or Mashvisor allow investors to quickly analyze prospective deals, calculating metrics like cash flow, cap rate, and return on investment (ROI) with ease.

A standardized approach to deal analysis ensures that each potential investment aligns with the investor's goals and financial criteria. By creating a checklist or scoring system that considers factors such as location, property condition, rental demand, and financing options, investors can assess deals objectively and avoid emotionally-driven decisions. Automated deal analysis software can streamline this process further, providing consistent metrics that make it easier to compare properties and identify those that offer the best long-term potential.

Investor and analyst Emily Jackson shares her approach: "I have alerts set up for new listings that fit my criteria, and I use a deal analysis tool to quickly assess each property. It saves me hours each week and ensures I'm only looking at deals that meet my investment standards." By automating lead generation and establishing a systematized approach to deal analysis, investors can scale their business more effectively, ensuring a steady pipeline of quality investment opportunities.

Laying the Foundation for Sustainable Growth

Building a strong foundation of systems and processes is the first step toward scaling a real estate business successfully. By streamlining property management, establishing efficient accounting practices, and automating lead generation and deal analysis, investors create a scalable infrastructure that supports long-term growth. These systems not only enhance operational efficiency but also reduce the risk of errors, improve tenant satisfaction, and enable investors to make data-driven decisions that benefit their portfolios.

As the business grows, a solid foundation of systems and processes provides stability, allowing investors to focus on strategy and expansion rather than being bogged down by day-to-day tasks. With an organized and efficient operation, investors are well-equipped to scale confidently, take on new opportunities, and ultimately build a robust, sustainable real estate portfolio.

Building a Team and Leveraging Outsourcing

As a real estate business grows, the need for specialized skills and additional support becomes essential. Scaling successfully means recognizing that a single person can't handle every aspect of property management, deal sourcing, and financial oversight. By building a reliable team and leveraging outsourcing for non-core tasks, investors free up valuable time to focus on strategy and expansion. A well-rounded team provides expertise in critical areas, while outsourcing allows flexibility and efficiency, helping investors manage an expanding portfolio without becoming overwhelmed.

Identifying Key Roles and Building a Core Team

The first step in building a scalable real estate business is assembling a team of professionals who bring expertise and reliability to essential functions. Key roles that support a growing portfolio include property managers, accountants, maintenance coordinators, and real estate agents. Property managers handle the day-to-day operations, including tenant interactions, rent collection, and property maintenance, allowing investors to step back from time-consuming tasks while ensuring that properties are well-managed.

Accountants play a crucial role in keeping finances organized, tracking expenses, handling tax obligations, and providing financial reports. Having a dedicated accountant who specializes in real estate can save both time and money, helping investors identify tax advantages and maintain accurate records. Additionally, a trusted maintenance coordinator or contractor ensures that properties are kept in top condition and that repairs are handled promptly, preserving asset value and tenant satisfaction.

Investor and business owner Laura Mason shares her experience with building a team: "My property manager, accountant, and maintenance coordinator are invaluable. They handle the day-to-day so I can focus on growing the business. I know I can trust them to take care of things, which gives me the confidence to expand." By establishing a core team, investors can delegate daily tasks to experienced professionals, allowing them to concentrate on scaling and strategic planning.

Leveraging Virtual Assistants and Specialized Support for Efficiency

For tasks that do not require full-time staff, virtual assistants (VAs) and freelance specialists provide an effective, flexible solution. VAs can handle a variety of administrative tasks, such as scheduling, data entry, and responding to tenant inquiries, while specialized freelancers can be hired for specific projects like graphic design for marketing materials, website updates, or digital marketing campaigns. Virtual assistants are cost-effective, allowing investors to scale administrative support up or down as needed without committing to a permanent hire.

In addition to virtual assistants, outsourcing specific functions such as bookkeeping, tenant screening, and legal support can enhance operational efficiency. Bookkeeping services can manage monthly accounting tasks, allowing the primary accountant to focus on high-level financial analysis and strategy. Similarly, outsourcing tenant screening to a specialized agency ensures that thorough background checks are conducted efficiently, reducing vacancy times and finding qualified tenants quickly. Legal support is also essential for tasks like lease drafting and eviction processes, ensuring that contracts are compliant with local regulations and reducing potential legal risks.

Real estate entrepreneur James Rizzo explains how outsourcing has helped him scale: "I have a VA who handles tenant inquiries and helps me stay organized, plus a few freelancers for things like bookkeeping and marketing. It's efficient and keeps overhead low while giving me access to quality work." Outsourcing allows investors to tap into specialized skills without the expense of hiring full-time employees, creating a flexible support network that grows alongside the business.

Building a Network of Trusted Partners

Beyond direct employees and outsourced staff, building relationships with reliable vendors and industry partners is essential to scaling a real estate business. Trusted contractors, lenders, insurance agents, and real estate agents form a valuable network that supports various aspects of property management and acquisition. For example, a dependable contractor who understands an investor's standards can handle renovations and repairs efficiently, maintaining property value and tenant satisfaction. Real estate agents with a deep knowledge of the local market can provide valuable insights into emerging trends, off-market deals, and pricing strategies, giving investors a competitive edge.

Lenders who specialize in real estate can offer financing options tailored to an investor's growth strategy, including portfolio loans and refinancing solutions that allow for expansion. Insurance agents familiar with real estate risks can help investors navigate policy options, ensuring properties are adequately covered against unexpected events. These partnerships save time, improve service quality, and reduce costs, enabling investors to operate with efficiency and confidence.

Experienced investor Sarah Fields highlights the importance of a solid network: "Having a team of reliable partners—from my contractors to my mortgage broker—makes all the difference. I know I can depend on them, which is crucial when you're managing multiple properties and scaling up." By fostering relationships with trusted partners, investors build a reliable support network that makes managing a growing portfolio easier and more effective.

Creating a Scalable, Resilient Business through Teamwork and Outsourcing

Scaling a real estate business successfully means recognizing the value of a strong team, effective outsourcing, and trusted partnerships. By assembling a core team to manage essential functions, utilizing virtual assistants and freelancers for flexible support, and building a network of dependable partners, investors can handle the demands of a larger portfolio without compromising on quality or efficiency. Delegating tasks strategically not only frees up time for growth-focused activities but also creates a resilient business structure that can handle the challenges of expansion.

With a well-organized team and support network, investors are better equipped to pursue new opportunities, manage properties effectively, and adapt to the needs of a growing business. By leveraging the skills of experienced professionals and outsourcing non-core tasks, investors create a scalable business model that positions them for long-term success in the competitive real estate market.

Expanding Through Strategic Financing and Partnerships

To scale a real estate business, access to capital is essential. Expanding a portfolio often requires funding beyond what traditional mortgages provide, which is why strategic financing and partnerships become vital tools for growth. By leveraging portfolio loans, private lending, and forming joint ventures with other investors, real estate entrepreneurs can unlock opportunities that might otherwise be out of reach. Creative financing and strategic partnerships enable investors to diversify their portfolios, share risk, and enter larger or more complex deals that enhance long-term profitability.

Leveraging Portfolio Loans and Creative Financing Options

One of the most effective ways to finance multiple properties as a business scales is through portfolio loans. Unlike conventional mortgages, which are typically limited to individual properties, portfolio loans allow investors to finance multiple properties under a single loan. This structure streamlines financing, consolidates payments, and often offers more flexible terms, making it easier to manage a growing portfolio. Portfolio loans are especially useful for investors with a substantial number of properties, as lenders base approvals on the portfolio's collective performance, creating options for those who might otherwise hit conventional lending limits.

In addition to portfolio loans, private lending provides another valuable source of capital. Private lenders, including individuals, real estate funds, or private equity groups, offer funding that can be structured to meet specific project needs, such as short-term loans for fix-and-flip projects or bridge loans for properties in transition. Private loans often come with higher interest rates than traditional loans but offer flexibility in terms, timelines, and approval processes. For investors pursuing time-sensitive deals or unique property types, private lending can be a powerful tool.

Real estate investor Alan Brooks highlights his experience with creative financing: "When I started scaling, I realized traditional loans just couldn't keep up with my needs. Portfolio loans and private lenders helped me finance multiple properties, so I didn't have to slow down. It's allowed me to stay competitive and keep expanding." By utilizing portfolio loans and private lending, investors gain access to the capital needed to scale while maintaining the flexibility to pursue diverse investment strategies.

Forming Joint Ventures to Share Risk and Resources

Joint ventures (JVs) are partnerships where two or more investors pool their resources, skills, and capital to undertake a larger or more complex real estate project than they could manage individually. In a JV, each partner contributes something unique—such as capital, property management expertise, or deal sourcing—and shares the profits and risks accordingly. This collaborative approach not only diversifies risk but also enables investors to enter larger deals, such as commercial properties, multi-family complexes, or development projects, which can offer substantial returns.

Joint ventures are particularly beneficial for investors who are scaling quickly but wish to limit their financial exposure on any single deal. By splitting costs and sharing responsibilities, JV partners can expand their portfolios without taking on all the associated risks. Additionally, partnering with investors who have complementary skills allows each participant to focus on their strengths, enhancing the efficiency and effectiveness of the project. For example, one partner might specialize in financing and acquisitions, while the other handles property management and operations, creating a balanced and capable team.

Developer Emily White shares her insights on JVs: "I've formed joint ventures with other investors on several projects, and it's been transformative for my business. Working with partners lets me take on deals I wouldn't tackle alone, and we share the financial burden. It's a great way to scale and build relationships with like-minded investors." By forming JVs, investors can expand their portfolios more rapidly, benefiting from shared expertise and resources while reducing individual risk.

Building Strategic Partnerships for Long-Term Growth

In addition to financial partnerships, strategic alliances with key industry players can support long-term growth. Relationships with contractors, property managers, brokers, and lenders provide essential support as a real estate business scales. For instance, partnering with a reliable contractor ensures timely and high-quality property renovations, which is crucial for flipping properties or repositioning rental units to attract higher-paying tenants. Working closely with brokers and agents who understand an investor's specific goals can also lead to off-market deals and favorable terms, giving investors an edge in competitive markets.

Developing strong relationships with local lenders and community banks offers another advantage. Smaller financial institutions often provide more flexible terms and a personalized approach, making it easier for investors to secure financing for unconventional or value-add projects. Additionally, forming long-term partnerships with these institutions can lead to quicker loan approvals and favorable refinancing options, supporting an investor's expansion goals.

Real estate entrepreneur Kevin Zhang emphasizes the importance of strategic partnerships: "My relationships with brokers, contractors, and lenders are key to scaling my business. They bring me deals, help me execute projects efficiently, and keep things moving smoothly. These partnerships are just as important as access to capital." Strategic partnerships provide the network and expertise necessary to handle the increased demands of a larger portfolio, making it possible for investors to grow sustainably and profitably.

Creating a Scalable Business with Capital and Collaboration

Expanding a real estate business through strategic financing and partnerships allows investors to access the resources, support, and expertise needed to grow confidently. By leveraging portfolio loans, private lending, joint ventures, and building partnerships with industry professionals, investors can pursue larger deals, diversify their portfolios, and manage growth effectively. These strategies not only provide the capital required to scale but also create a resilient business model that thrives on collaboration and shared expertise.

Scaling a real estate business is challenging, but with the right financing options and strategic partnerships, investors can achieve sustainable growth while reducing risk and maintaining financial stability. By aligning with partners who bring complementary skills and capital, real estate investors create a scalable, well-supported business that can adapt to opportunities in any market condition. This collaborative approach to growth ensures that investors can continue expanding their portfolios and achieving long-term success in the dynamic world of real estate.

Chapter 21

Chapter 21: Real Estate Law and Compliance

Understanding Zoning, Land Use, and Property Rights

Zoning laws, land use regulations, and property rights form the backbone of real estate law, dictating what investors can and cannot do with their properties. A thorough understanding of these laws is essential for any real estate investor, as they directly influence property value, development potential, and long-term investment viability. By familiarizing themselves with zoning classifications, land use restrictions, property boundaries, and other key elements of property rights, investors can make more informed decisions and avoid costly legal issues.

The Basics of Zoning and Land Use Classifications

Zoning laws are local or municipal regulations that determine how land within a specific area can be used. Typically, properties are classified under various zoning categories—such as residential, commercial, industrial, or agricultural—each with its own set of rules governing permissible uses. For example, a property zoned for residential use may restrict commercial activities, while commercial zoning might permit retail businesses but not industrial operations. Zoning can even get more specific within each category, with subcategories like single-family residential or multi-family residential, which further limit the types of structures allowed.

Understanding the zoning classification of a property is crucial for investors because it influences what they can build or operate on the site. For instance, if an investor intends to open a small café but the property is zoned for residential use, they would likely need to seek a zoning variance or rezoning approval to legally operate a business. Such approvals, however, are not guaranteed and can be time-consuming and costly. Investors should check zoning codes early in the acquisition process to ensure their intended use aligns with local regulations or be prepared to go through the proper channels to seek modifications.

Real estate attorney Sarah Lee emphasizes the importance of zoning knowledge: "Zoning restrictions can make or break a deal. Investors need to confirm that a property's zoning aligns with their vision before they invest. Otherwise, they may face legal battles or costly delays." A solid grasp of zoning ensures that investors select properties suited to their plans, reducing the risk of unforeseen complications.

Navigating Land Use Restrictions and Easements

Beyond zoning, various land use restrictions govern how properties can be developed and modified. Local governments may impose height restrictions, lot size requirements, and density limits, all of which impact development potential. Additionally, certain areas may have aesthetic or environmental requirements, particularly in historically significant neighborhoods or environmentally sensitive zones. For example, a city may impose guidelines on building design in historic districts to preserve architectural integrity or restrict development near waterways to protect natural habitats.

Easements are another critical aspect of land use that investors need to consider. An easement is a legal right granted to a third party to use a portion of the property for a specific purpose, such as access to utilities, roadways, or neighboring land. Easements can impact the usability of a property and may limit an investor's ability to develop certain areas. For instance, a utility easement running through a lot might restrict the construction of buildings or structures in that area. Easements are typically recorded in public land records, and investors should review these records to understand any encumbrances that might affect their property rights.

Surveyor and land use consultant James Cooper explains, "I always recommend that investors obtain a thorough land survey and title search before closing. Easements and other land use restrictions can be hidden obstacles, and knowing about them upfront can save investors from future headaches." Understanding land use restrictions and easements allows investors to assess properties fully and plan developments that comply with local laws and avoid potential conflicts.

Conducting Title Searches and Ensuring Clear Property Boundaries

One of the most fundamental steps in any property transaction is conducting a title search to verify property ownership and ensure clear title. A title search investigates the history of a property's ownership, identifying any existing claims, liens, or encumbrances that could affect the buyer's ownership rights. A clean title, free from liens and disputes, is essential for investors seeking to avoid potential legal complications after acquisition. Issues like unpaid property taxes, outstanding mortgages, or inheritance claims can impact a property's title, and resolving these matters can delay closing or lead to unexpected costs.

Investors should also confirm property boundaries through a survey. Property boundaries define the exact lines of ownership, clarifying where one property ends and another begins. This is especially important for properties with potential for development, as encroaching on neighboring land, even unintentionally, can lead to disputes or costly adjustments. Surveys can also reveal any discrepancies between actual property boundaries and what is recorded in public documents, allowing investors to address these issues before they become problematic.

Title insurance is another key safeguard, protecting buyers from potential losses due to title defects that may arise after the purchase. By securing title insurance, investors reduce their financial risk and gain peace of mind, knowing that their ownership rights are protected against future claims.

Real estate advisor Laura Gibson highlights the importance of due diligence: "I tell my clients to invest in a comprehensive title search and boundary survey for every property. These steps might seem tedious, but they prevent costly surprises down the road." By conducting thorough title searches and verifying property boundaries, investors protect their rights, ensure clear ownership, and avoid legal disputes that could hinder their investment.

Building Confidence Through Legal Knowledge

Zoning, land use, and property rights are foundational elements of real estate law that every investor must understand to navigate the market successfully. From confirming that zoning aligns with intended property use to uncovering potential encumbrances through title searches, these legal considerations play a central role in determining a property's value and investment potential. By educating themselves on these topics and working with experienced professionals, investors can make informed decisions, comply with local regulations, and reduce the likelihood of unexpected legal challenges.

A strong understanding of zoning, land use, and property rights equips investors to identify properties that meet their criteria, develop projects confidently, and build a portfolio that aligns with their long-term goals. By approaching real estate investments with a comprehensive knowledge of these legal principles, investors can navigate the complexities of property law and ensure that each acquisition supports sustainable growth and profitability.

Navigating Landlord-Tenant Laws and Rental Property Compliance

For real estate investors in the rental market, understanding landlord-tenant laws and complying with rental property regulations are essential for a successful and legally sound business. These laws govern every aspect of the landlord-tenant relationship, from lease agreements to tenant rights, maintenance responsibilities, and eviction procedures. By staying informed on landlord-tenant laws and ensuring rental property compliance, investors can reduce the risk of disputes, create a fair experience for tenants, and protect their business from costly legal challenges.

Drafting and Enforcing Lease Agreements

The lease agreement is the foundation of the landlord-tenant relationship, outlining the terms under which a tenant rents the property. A well-crafted lease sets clear expectations for both parties, covering essential elements such as rent amount, due dates, security deposits, maintenance responsibilities, and rules regarding property use. By creating a comprehensive and legally compliant lease, landlords can prevent misunderstandings and ensure that all policies are communicated transparently from the beginning.

Each state has specific requirements regarding lease agreements, and investors should tailor their leases to meet these requirements. For example, some states mandate specific disclosures, such as information on lead-based paint for properties built before 1978, while others may have specific language requirements for lease clauses. Many investors choose to work with a real estate attorney to ensure their lease agreements comply with state laws, as even small errors can lead to legal issues if a dispute arises.

In addition to drafting the lease, landlords must enforce its terms consistently and fairly. For instance, if a lease specifies a late fee for overdue rent, it is essential to apply this policy uniformly across all tenants. Selective enforcement can be perceived as favoritism or discrimination, potentially leading to legal challenges. Real estate investor Rachel Moore emphasizes the importance of consistency: "A clear, consistent lease policy keeps things fair for everyone. When tenants know the rules and see that they're enforced uniformly, it creates a respectful and stable relationship."

Understanding Tenant Rights and Fair Housing Laws

Tenant rights vary by state but generally include the right to a safe, habitable living environment, protection from discrimination, and the right to privacy. As landlords, investors have a legal obligation to respect these rights, ensuring that properties are well-maintained, accessible, and compliant with local housing codes. A failure to meet these obligations can lead to legal actions, fines, and potential damages for violating tenant rights.

Fair housing laws, established under the Fair Housing Act, protect tenants from discrimination based on race, color, national origin, religion, sex, familial status, and disability. Landlords must avoid discriminatory practices when advertising properties, screening tenants, and setting rental terms. For example, it is illegal to refuse to rent to a tenant based on their family status or to charge higher rent based on gender or ethnicity. Compliance with fair housing laws is not only a legal requirement but also essential for building an inclusive and respectful tenant community.

Investors should also be aware of reasonable accommodation laws, which require landlords to make necessary modifications or adjustments to accommodate tenants with disabilities. This could include allowing a service animal in a no-pet property or permitting minor property modifications, such as grab bars in bathrooms. Fair housing compliance protects landlords from discrimination claims and ensures that tenants feel secure and respected within their rental community.

Real estate attorney Linda Green emphasizes the importance of fair housing awareness: "Landlords who understand fair housing laws and take proactive steps to comply not only avoid legal issues but also foster a positive, inclusive environment. It's good for business and builds trust with tenants." By respecting tenant rights and adhering to fair housing laws, investors create a fair and compliant rental experience that benefits both tenants and the business.

Maintenance Obligations and Habitability Standards

One of the most important responsibilities of a landlord is to provide a safe and habitable property. Habitability standards, which vary by state and municipality, require landlords to ensure that essential services, such as heating, plumbing, and electrical systems, are functional and that properties are free from health and safety hazards. Common requirements include providing hot water, safe stairways, secure windows and doors, and addressing issues like mold, pest infestations, and lead paint in older buildings.

Promptly addressing maintenance requests is essential for complying with habitability standards and maintaining positive tenant relationships. When tenants report issues, such as a broken heater or leaky faucet, landlords must respond within a reasonable timeframe. Regular property inspections and preventive maintenance can help landlords stay ahead of repairs, ensuring that the property remains in good condition and that potential problems are resolved before they become serious.

Many landlords establish a process for handling maintenance requests, using property management software or online portals where tenants can submit issues and track progress. This system not only improves efficiency but also provides documentation in case of disputes. Some investors choose to work with property management companies to handle maintenance, ensuring that repairs are managed professionally and on time.

Property manager and investor Tom Davis shares his approach to maintenance: "Quick response to maintenance requests is essential for tenant satisfaction and compliance. I keep my properties on a regular maintenance schedule and document every request to stay on top of things. It keeps tenants happy and ensures my properties are always in great shape." By prioritizing maintenance and habitability, landlords meet legal requirements, protect property value, and foster positive tenant relationships.

Building a Compliant and Respectful Landlord-Tenant Relationship

Navigating landlord-tenant laws and ensuring rental property compliance are key to managing a successful rental business. From drafting clear lease agreements to respecting tenant rights and meeting habitability standards, these responsibilities help landlords avoid legal challenges, create a positive rental experience, and protect their investments. Staying informed on current landlord-tenant laws, consulting with legal professionals, and consistently applying best practices in property management enable investors to build a reputation as fair and responsible landlords.

By respecting the legal framework governing rental properties, investors create a compliant, respectful environment that promotes tenant satisfaction and stability. A proactive approach to legal compliance not only reduces the risk of disputes and fines but also strengthens the business, contributing to long-term success in the rental market.

Contracts, Disclosure Obligations, and Real Estate Transactions

In real estate, contracts, disclosure obligations, and transactional compliance are essential to the integrity and security of every deal. Whether buying, selling, or leasing a property, understanding the legal requirements in contracts and disclosures helps investors avoid disputes, protect their interests, and ensure smooth transactions. A clear understanding of real estate contracts, the importance of due diligence, and mandatory disclosure laws equips investors to handle transactions confidently and responsibly.

Drafting and Reviewing Real Estate Contracts

Real estate contracts are legally binding agreements that outline the terms of a property transaction, from purchase agreements to lease and option contracts. Each contract should clearly define the rights and responsibilities of all parties involved, as well as the terms under which the property will be transferred, leased, or sold. Key elements typically include the purchase price, closing date, contingencies, inspection periods, and any special conditions or requirements.

For investors, it's essential to review contracts carefully or consult a real estate attorney to ensure that all terms are fair, enforceable, and aligned with their goals. Even seemingly small details, such as deadlines for inspections or conditions for loan approvals, can have significant financial implications if overlooked. Well-drafted contracts not only provide legal protection but also clarify expectations for all parties, reducing the likelihood of misunderstandings and disputes.

Real estate investor Michael Johnson highlights the importance of thorough contract review: "Contracts are complex, and any oversight can be costly. I always have my attorney review every agreement, no matter how straightforward it seems. It's better to address potential issues upfront than to face disputes later." A well-drafted contract offers clarity, legal protection, and peace of mind, allowing investors to proceed with transactions confidently.

Conducting Due Diligence in Property Transactions

Due diligence is the process of investigating a property to assess its condition, value, and compliance with applicable regulations before finalizing a purchase. This process includes property inspections, title searches, environmental assessments, and financial reviews, ensuring that investors have a complete understanding of the property they are acquiring. Due diligence protects buyers from unexpected liabilities, helping them avoid properties with hidden issues that could compromise profitability.

A title search, for example, verifies property ownership and identifies any encumbrances, such as liens, easements, or boundary disputes, that could affect ownership rights. Similarly, property inspections assess the physical condition of the property, uncovering potential issues like structural damage, outdated systems, or code violations. Environmental assessments, often required for commercial properties, check for contamination risks that could lead to regulatory fines or cleanup costs.

Real estate advisor Susan Moore explains the value of due diligence: "Due diligence is non-negotiable. It's the only way to truly know what you're buying and to negotiate from a position of strength. Skipping this step can result in costly surprises that could have been avoided." By conducting thorough due diligence, investors mitigate risks, make informed decisions, and have greater negotiating power to adjust terms or address issues discovered during the review process.

Understanding Disclosure Obligations and Avoiding Liability

Disclosure laws require sellers and landlords to inform buyers or tenants of any known property defects or hazards that could impact their decision to proceed with the transaction. Common disclosures include information on structural issues, water damage, past repairs, environmental hazards, and neighborhood conditions. In residential transactions, disclosures are typically mandatory, while commercial disclosure requirements may vary depending on local regulations and the nature of the transaction.

Failure to disclose known defects can lead to significant legal liabilities for sellers and landlords. If a buyer or tenant discovers an undisclosed issue after the transaction, they may file a lawsuit for damages or attempt to rescind the agreement. Disclosure forms are often used to document any issues and provide evidence that the seller or landlord has met their obligations. By completing disclosures accurately and transparently, sellers protect themselves from future claims and foster trust with the buyer or tenant.

Real estate attorney Jennifer Lopez advises her clients on the importance of full disclosure: "Transparency is key. If you know of an issue, disclose it. Trying to hide problems usually backfires, and the costs of a legal dispute far outweigh any short-term benefit from omitting information." Meeting disclosure obligations not only keeps investors compliant with the law but also strengthens their reputation as trustworthy and responsible professionals.

Ensuring Compliance in Real Estate Transactions

Contracts, due diligence, and disclosures are the cornerstones of compliance in real estate transactions. By understanding the legal requirements for each of these elements, investors protect their interests and build a solid foundation for their investments. Clear, well-structured contracts provide enforceable terms, due diligence reduces risk by uncovering potential issues, and accurate disclosures prevent liability by fostering transparency.

For real estate investors, navigating these legal responsibilities thoughtfully creates a more secure and stable business. With comprehensive knowledge of contract law, a commitment to thorough due diligence, and transparency in disclosures, investors can pursue real estate transactions with confidence, ensuring that each deal aligns with their goals and complies with all legal standards. By prioritizing legal integrity, investors not only protect their current investments but also lay the groundwork for sustainable, long-term success in the real estate market.

Chapter 22: Mentorship and Continuing Education

The Value of Mentorship in Real Estate Growth

Mentorship is one of the most powerful resources for growth in real estate. Having a mentor provides access to seasoned guidance, real-world insights, and invaluable feedback, allowing investors to accelerate their learning curve and avoid costly mistakes. Mentors offer advice grounded in experience, helping mentees navigate complex transactions, understand market dynamics, and refine their investment strategies. Whether an investor is just starting out or is looking to advance to the next level, mentorship can provide the support and perspective needed to achieve ambitious goals.

Finding the Right Mentor

Finding the right mentor is essential for a productive and enriching mentorship relationship. The ideal mentor should not only be experienced but should also align with the mentee's goals and values. For instance, a residential real estate investor may seek a mentor with expertise in single-family properties, while a commercial investor may prefer someone with experience in multifamily or retail properties. Choosing a mentor who understands a mentee's area of focus ensures that guidance is relevant and tailored to their specific needs.

When selecting a mentor, it's also important to consider their approach to teaching and feedback. A good mentor is someone who provides constructive criticism, challenges assumptions, and encourages growth, rather than simply validating ideas. Many successful investors attribute their growth to mentors who were willing to push them outside their comfort zones. Mentors should be available and willing to invest time in the relationship, whether that means regular check-ins, answering questions, or reviewing deals.

Finding a mentor may require networking, attending real estate events, or joining professional associations. Local real estate investment groups, online forums, and social media platforms like LinkedIn can also be valuable resources for connecting with experienced investors. Building a mentorship relationship is often a gradual process, and it may require reaching out to several potential mentors before finding a good fit.

Real estate investor Anna Fields shares her experience with finding a mentor: "I reached out to a few experienced investors in my area, asking for advice on specific projects. One of them offered ongoing support, and over time, our relationship developed into a mentorship. He's been instrumental in helping me scale my business and avoid common pitfalls." Taking the time to find the right mentor can lead to a mutually beneficial relationship that enhances both personal and professional growth.

Building and Maintaining a Productive Mentor-Mentee Relationship

A successful mentorship requires commitment and active engagement from both the mentor and mentee. For mentees, it's essential to approach the relationship with respect, openness, and a willingness to learn. This means listening carefully, implementing feedback, and showing appreciation for the mentor's time and expertise. Setting clear expectations and goals from the start can help guide the relationship and ensure both parties are aligned in terms of what they hope to achieve.

Regular communication is also key. Mentees should schedule periodic check-ins to discuss progress, seek advice on new challenges, and update mentors on their accomplishments. Rather than waiting for the mentor to reach out, mentees should take the initiative in arranging meetings, sending updates, and asking questions. This proactive approach demonstrates commitment and respect for the mentor's time, encouraging them to stay engaged in the relationship.

Mentorship is not only about receiving guidance but also about building a genuine connection. Showing appreciation, whether through a thank-you note, acknowledging their support publicly, or offering to help with a project, can strengthen the bond. Many mentorship relationships evolve into long-term professional connections, with mentors often becoming trusted advisors or even future partners in deals.

Property manager and mentor David Lee emphasizes the importance of a strong mentor-mentee connection: "Some of my most rewarding relationships are with people I've mentored over the years. The ones who make the most progress are those who actively engage, ask questions, and stay in touch. It becomes more than just mentorship—it's a partnership." By nurturing the relationship, mentees can create a supportive network that benefits their career well beyond the initial mentorship period.

The Benefits of Mentorship for Real Estate Investors

The value of mentorship extends far beyond immediate advice—it's a resource that can shape an investor's mindset, broaden their network, and open doors to new opportunities.

Mentors can introduce mentees to industry contacts, from lenders to contractors, who can provide valuable support as their portfolio grows. Additionally, a mentor's perspective helps mentees make sound decisions based on experience, reducing the likelihood of costly errors and building confidence.

For novice investors, mentorship can shorten the learning curve, transforming theoretical knowledge into practical skills. Mentors can guide mentees through their first few deals, pointing out potential red flags and teaching them to evaluate properties, negotiate terms, and manage risks effectively. For seasoned investors, mentorship can provide fresh insights and help them explore new strategies, markets, or property types they may not have considered before.

Investor Tom Rivera shares how mentorship transformed his career: "Having a mentor gave me the confidence to take on bigger deals. He helped me understand market cycles, the importance of due diligence, and how to build a network. I wouldn't be where I am today without his guidance." With a mentor's support, investors at any stage can expand their knowledge, grow their portfolios, and achieve new levels of success in the real estate industry.

Unlocking Potential Through Mentorship

In real estate, mentorship is an invaluable tool for personal and professional growth. By finding the right mentor, building a strong relationship, and actively engaging in the learning process, investors gain access to expertise and support that can accelerate their journey to success. Mentors provide more than just knowledge—they offer a blueprint for overcoming challenges, seizing opportunities, and achieving long-term goals in the competitive world of real estate.

For those willing to invest in mentorship, the rewards can be transformative. The guidance, connections, and confidence gained through mentorship create a solid foundation for sustainable growth and continuous improvement, empowering investors to navigate the real estate industry with clarity and purpose.

Staying Updated on Market Trends and Industry Changes

In real estate, knowledge is power. The industry is dynamic, with market conditions, regulatory environments, and economic factors constantly shifting. For investors, staying informed about current market trends, economic shifts, and industry developments is crucial for making strategic decisions and maintaining a competitive edge. By adopting habits that keep them up-to-date, investors can identify new opportunities, mitigate risks, and adapt their strategies to align with changes in the real estate landscape.

Understanding Market Trends and Economic Indicators

Real estate markets are influenced by a wide range of economic indicators, from interest rates and inflation to employment rates and consumer spending. These factors affect property values, demand for housing, and rental rates, making it essential for investors to understand how they impact the market. For example, when interest rates are low, borrowing becomes more affordable, increasing buyer demand and often driving up property prices. Conversely, rising interest rates can reduce affordability, slowing down the market and creating buying opportunities for investors who can leverage cash reserves.

Staying informed on national and local economic trends is critical, as real estate is highly localized. In addition to broad economic indicators, investors should track factors specific to their target markets, such as population growth, job market conditions, and infrastructure developments. For example, if a city is experiencing rapid job growth and an influx of new residents, it may signal increased demand for housing, making it a prime area for investment. Conversely, markets that are seeing population declines or industry downturns may warrant caution.

Economist and real estate advisor Jennifer Li explains the importance of tracking economic trends: "Markets are cyclical, and understanding where we are in the economic cycle can help investors make more informed decisions. By keeping an eye on leading indicators, like employment and interest rates, investors can anticipate market changes and adjust accordingly." With a keen understanding of economic indicators, investors can time their acquisitions, sales, and strategies to maximize profitability and minimize risk.

Using Resources to Stay Informed on Real Estate Developments

Staying updated requires access to reliable information sources. Industry publications, local market reports, and economic forecasts provide valuable insights into current trends and emerging opportunities. Subscribing to real estate magazines, such as *REALTOR® Magazine*, *Real Estate Weekly*, or *Multi-Housing News*, offers up-to-date news, expert insights, and data-driven analysis. Local real estate boards and economic development agencies also publish periodic reports that highlight trends specific to regional markets, including price changes, vacancy rates, and new construction.

Online platforms and news aggregators like *BiggerPockets*, *Investopedia*, and *REtipster* offer a wealth of information tailored to real estate investors. Many of these sites also feature forums where investors can discuss market trends, share experiences, and learn from one another. Following industry experts and economists on social media platforms like LinkedIn and Twitter provides real-time updates on market trends, policy changes, and investment strategies.

Attending real estate seminars, webinars, and conferences is another effective way to stay informed and build connections with industry professionals. Many events feature panels and presentations by leading economists, real estate investors, and market analysts who provide valuable insights into trends and predictions. Networking with other attendees can also open doors to new opportunities, partnerships, and investment ideas.

Investor Michelle Parks emphasizes the value of these resources: "I read local market reports monthly, follow industry experts, and attend at least two conferences a year. It keeps me in tune with what's happening, and it's invaluable for making informed decisions." By incorporating various resources into their routine, investors gain a well-rounded view of the market, enabling them to spot trends early and adapt their strategies.

Recognizing the Impact of Regulatory and Policy Changes

Regulations and policies play a critical role in real estate, affecting everything from financing and tax benefits to zoning laws and landlord-tenant regulations. Staying updated on regulatory changes ensures that investors remain compliant with the law and can take advantage of any new benefits or incentives. For example, changes in tax laws, such as the introduction of new deductions or changes to capital gains tax rates, can significantly impact real estate profitability. Investors should be proactive in understanding how these changes affect their portfolios and in adapting their strategies accordingly.

New policies on housing affordability, rent control, and property development can also impact investment decisions. For example, the implementation of rent control laws in some cities may limit rental income potential, making certain markets less attractive for investors focused on cash flow. Conversely, government incentives for affordable housing or tax breaks for green building initiatives could present new opportunities in specific regions or property types.

Working with legal and financial advisors who specialize in real estate can help investors navigate the complex landscape of real estate regulations. These professionals can provide guidance on compliance and keep investors informed about upcoming changes that could affect their investments. Real estate attorney Greg Nelson emphasizes the importance of staying informed on policy changes: "Regulations can shift quickly, especially with zoning and rental laws. Investors who stay updated can navigate these changes effectively, while those who don't may face compliance issues or miss out on new opportunities." By staying informed on regulatory shifts, investors ensure their portfolios remain compliant and are well-positioned to benefit from any new policies.

Empowering Strategic Decisions Through Knowledge

In an industry as dynamic as real estate, staying informed is a competitive advantage. By understanding economic indicators, leveraging reliable information sources, and monitoring regulatory changes, investors empower themselves to make well-informed, strategic decisions. These habits allow investors to adapt to market cycles, capitalize on emerging opportunities, and mitigate risks in a changing landscape.

Regularly staying updated on market trends and industry changes is more than just a best practice—it's a vital part of building a resilient, profitable real estate portfolio. With a commitment to continuous learning and awareness, investors can navigate the real estate market with confidence, ensuring that each decision is backed by current data and insights.

Investing in Real Estate Education and Skill Development

In a competitive and ever-evolving industry, continuous education and skill development are crucial for real estate investors who want to excel and maintain a competitive edge. Formal education, industry certifications, and skill-building courses equip investors with the tools and knowledge needed to manage complex deals, analyze investments accurately, and navigate market challenges confidently. By committing to lifelong learning, investors not only deepen their expertise but also enhance their adaptability, ensuring sustained success in a dynamic market.

Pursuing Industry Certifications and Specialized Courses

Industry certifications provide structured education that focuses on specific aspects of real estate, such as property analysis, market research, finance, and property management. Certifications such as the Certified Commercial Investment Member (CCIM), Certified Property Manager (CPM), and Real Estate Investment Analyst (REIA) are widely recognized in the industry and demonstrate a high level of expertise. These credentials signal to clients, partners, and investors that an individual has undergone rigorous training and mastered advanced skills, making them more competitive and trusted in the marketplace.

Each certification program typically covers core areas essential to real estate success. For example, the CCIM designation emphasizes investment analysis, financial modeling, and market analysis for commercial properties, while the CPM focuses on property management best practices, tenant relations, and building operations. Many certification programs also require continuing education to maintain the designation, ensuring that certified professionals stay current on industry developments and best practices.

In addition to certifications, specialized courses—often available through real estate organizations, local community colleges, or online learning platforms—provide in-depth knowledge on specific skills. Topics such as negotiation, due diligence, and real estate finance are valuable for investors seeking targeted training. Platforms like Udemy, Coursera, and LinkedIn Learning offer affordable, accessible courses taught by experienced industry professionals, allowing investors to learn at their own pace.

Investor and property manager Lisa Cheng shares her experience with certifications: "Getting my CCIM was a game-changer. The training expanded my skills in financial analysis and market research, and I apply what I learned every day. It's an investment in yourself that pays off in better deals and more opportunities." By pursuing certifications and courses, investors can sharpen their skills and demonstrate a commitment to professionalism and excellence.

Joining Professional Organizations and Real Estate Networks

Professional organizations like the National Association of Realtors (NAR), Urban Land Institute (ULI), and local real estate investor associations offer members access to ongoing education, networking events, and industry resources. These organizations regularly host seminars, webinars, and conferences on topics ranging from market trends to legal updates, allowing investors to stay informed on best practices and emerging developments.

Joining a professional organization not only provides educational benefits but also offers networking opportunities with industry experts and peers. Many organizations also provide members with access to research reports, legal resources, and investment tools that support decision-making and strategic planning. Additionally, some associations offer mentorship programs or exclusive online forums where members can ask questions, discuss strategies, and learn from one another.

Real estate consultant Mark Davis highlights the value of industry associations: "Membership in professional organizations has helped me connect with top investors and stay updated on best practices. The educational resources and networking opportunities are invaluable—they keep you sharp and plugged into the industry." By joining professional networks, investors gain access to ongoing learning and support, enabling them to keep pace with the latest trends and insights.

Enhancing Key Skills Through Practical Experience

While formal education is valuable, nothing beats hands-on experience when it comes to mastering real estate. Practical experience helps investors develop critical skills such as deal analysis, negotiation, and property management in real-world scenarios. Each transaction, tenant interaction, and property acquisition adds to an investor's knowledge base, providing insights that can't be gained solely from textbooks or classrooms. By actively participating in the market, investors learn to anticipate challenges, evaluate properties more accurately, and make quick, informed decisions.

Mentorship and partnerships also offer valuable experiential learning. Working alongside experienced investors allows newer investors to gain firsthand exposure to complex deals, understand risk management, and witness negotiation tactics in action. For example, partnering on a deal or shadowing a mentor provides insights into the intricacies of contract terms, closing procedures, and managing unexpected obstacles, building confidence and competence over time.

Investor Jonathan Hayes emphasizes the importance of practical experience: "I learned so much more from my first few deals than I ever could in a classroom. Making real decisions, handling negotiations, and working through challenges taught me how to adapt and improve with each project." Hands-on experience reinforces theoretical knowledge, helping investors develop the practical skills needed to succeed in the competitive world of real estate.

Building a Foundation for Lifelong Success

Education and skill development are vital components of a successful real estate career. By investing in certifications, joining professional organizations, and gaining practical experience, investors build a solid foundation of knowledge and skills that enhance their decision-making, credibility, and adaptability. A commitment to lifelong learning not only strengthens an investor's abilities but also fosters resilience, preparing them to navigate both market challenges and opportunities.

In the fast-paced world of real estate, continuous education is not merely an advantage; it's a necessity. Staying educated and honing one's skills allows investors to grow sustainably, take on more complex projects, and elevate their careers. With the right mix of formal education, industry involvement, and practical experience, investors can confidently tackle any real estate challenge, knowing they are equipped to thrive in a constantly evolving industry.

Chapter 23: Lessons from Failure

Recognizing Common Real Estate Mistakes and Learning from Them

In real estate, even the most experienced investors make mistakes. The industry's complexity, combined with ever-changing market dynamics, means that setbacks are an inevitable part of the journey. However, each mistake holds a valuable lesson that can strengthen an investor's decision-making and strategy. By understanding some of the most common mistakes in real estate—and the lessons they teach—investors can better anticipate potential pitfalls, avoid repeating similar errors, and ultimately build a more resilient business.

Underestimating Renovation and Maintenance Costs

One of the most frequent mistakes in real estate is underestimating the costs associated with property renovations and maintenance. Many investors overlook key expenses during initial calculations, assuming that they can complete renovations quickly and inexpensively. However, once the project begins, unexpected costs often arise, from hidden structural issues to rising material prices or contractor delays. These unforeseen expenses can rapidly erode profit margins, leaving investors with less-than-expected returns or even losses.

For example, an investor purchasing a fixer-upper may budget $20,000 for repairs, only to find that outdated wiring, plumbing issues, or unforeseen code violations add another $10,000 to the project cost. Similarly, properties in older neighborhoods may require higher ongoing maintenance, leading to additional expenses that weren't accounted for during initial planning.

Real estate investor Steve Larson shares his experience: "My first rehab project went way over budget because I didn't anticipate the true scope of work. I learned the hard way to budget extra for surprises. Now, I always add a 20% contingency to my renovation budget." By acknowledging the potential for unexpected expenses, investors can build a financial cushion into their budgets, ensuring they are prepared for surprises and can complete projects without stretching their resources.

Overlooking Due Diligence and Property Research

Another common mistake in real estate is rushing through due diligence and property research. Thorough research—on both the property and the surrounding market—is essential for making informed investment decisions. Skipping due diligence, such as inspecting the property, verifying title records, or analyzing the local rental market, can lead to costly oversights. For instance, an investor who purchases a property without conducting a thorough inspection may later discover extensive damage, zoning restrictions, or title issues that require expensive remediation or limit the property's intended use.

Proper due diligence goes beyond physical inspections; it also includes researching the neighborhood and understanding market trends. Investors who neglect this research may invest in areas with declining property values, high vacancy rates, or lack of demand for rentals. By taking the time to gather relevant information, investors reduce the risk of surprises that could impact profitability or delay project timelines.

Real estate consultant Rachel Kim advises investors to prioritize due diligence: "Due diligence is non-negotiable. Rushing through it is like buying a property blindfolded. Even if it's a hot deal, taking the time to investigate will save you from bigger problems later." By being thorough in their research, investors can approach each property with a clear understanding of both the risks and opportunities it presents, avoiding issues that might derail their investment goals.

Misjudging Market Timing and Overleveraging

Timing plays a significant role in real estate, as market cycles affect property values, rental demand, and interest rates. A common mistake investors make is misjudging the timing of their purchases, either by buying in an overheated market or expecting quick returns in a slow market. Buying at the peak of a market cycle can result in losses if property values decline, while selling in a down market may lead to missed profits when values rebound. Successful investors learn to recognize market signals, such as rising interest rates or increasing inventory, which can indicate an impending shift in market conditions.

Overleveraging—taking on too much debt relative to one's cash flow—is another common misstep. Many investors are tempted to maximize their borrowing potential to expand their portfolios quickly. However, overleveraging leaves investors vulnerable to cash flow issues, especially if rental income decreases, interest rates rise, or unexpected expenses arise. Investors with high debt levels may struggle to cover their mortgage payments during a downturn, potentially leading to foreclosure or forced sales.

Investor Tom Grant shares his experience with overleveraging: "I expanded too quickly, relying heavily on loans. When the rental market slowed down, I found myself stretched thin. It was a tough lesson, but it taught me to be more cautious with debt." By managing debt conservatively and focusing on cash flow stability, investors can reduce the risks associated with high leverage, ensuring they can weather economic fluctuations.

Learning from Mistakes to Build a Stronger Business

Each of these common mistakes—underestimating renovation costs, skipping due diligence, and overleveraging—provides a valuable learning opportunity for investors. By recognizing these pitfalls, investors can implement strategies to avoid them, such as creating detailed budgets, conducting thorough property and market research, and using conservative financing. Mistakes are an inevitable part of any investment journey, but by approaching each setback as a lesson, investors strengthen their knowledge, resilience, and decision-making abilities.

Real estate is a field where continuous improvement is key. Learning from mistakes not only helps investors avoid costly errors but also instills a mindset focused on growth, preparation, and adaptability. By turning each failure into a stepping stone, investors can develop the skills and insights needed to build a successful, sustainable real estate business.

Embracing Resilience and Adapting Strategies

Resilience is a cornerstone of success in real estate investing. Markets fluctuate, projects don't always go as planned, and setbacks are inevitable, especially in an industry as complex and dynamic as real estate. For investors, the key to long-term success is not just avoiding failure but learning how to adapt, pivot, and persevere when things go wrong. By building resilience and embracing adaptability, investors can transform setbacks into growth opportunities and strengthen their ability to navigate future challenges.

Reassessing Goals and Realigning Strategies

When faced with a setback, the first step is often to reassess and realign. This may mean taking a closer look at the initial goals, re-evaluating the strategy, and adjusting expectations. For example, an investor who initially focused on flipping properties for quick returns may find the strategy unsustainable in a slow market or during a downturn. Rather than abandoning the investment, they might consider shifting their approach to long-term rentals or value-add investments, which can generate stable cash flow until market conditions improve.

Reassessing goals allows investors to take a broader view, identifying areas where they may have been overly optimistic or inflexible. Perhaps the initial focus was on aggressive growth, but after encountering market volatility or unexpected expenses, the investor realizes the need for a more conservative approach. By setting realistic expectations and making adjustments to align with current conditions, investors can create a more sustainable strategy that balances growth with stability.

Real estate advisor Laura Michaels shares her approach to setbacks: "When something doesn't go as planned, I see it as a chance to pivot and learn. Sometimes, the market or the property isn't what you expected. That's when you adapt—adjust your goals, refine your strategy, and keep moving forward." Embracing a flexible mindset helps investors stay focused on long-term success, even when immediate results don't meet their expectations.

Learning from Feedback and Cultivating a Growth Mindset

A growth mindset is essential for turning failures into learning experiences. This mindset encourages investors to view setbacks not as signs of inadequacy but as opportunities for improvement. By being open to feedback, whether from mentors, market data, or past experiences, investors gain insights into areas where they can enhance their skills, knowledge, or processes. A willingness to learn and improve empowers investors to approach each new challenge with confidence, knowing that they are better prepared than before.

Seeking feedback from trusted advisors or industry peers can provide fresh perspectives on what went wrong and how to prevent similar issues in the future. For example, an investor who misjudged market demand might consult with a mentor or attend industry workshops to better understand market analysis techniques. By actively seeking to learn from mistakes, investors strengthen their abilities and become more adept at anticipating potential pitfalls.

Investor Mark Sanchez reflects on his experience with learning from feedback: "Early in my career, I made some costly mistakes. Instead of letting them discourage me, I reached out to my mentor and asked what I could do better. His guidance and the lessons I took from those failures completely changed how I approach deals now." By valuing feedback and viewing challenges as learning experiences, investors develop resilience that sustains them through ups and downs.

Viewing Challenges as Opportunities for Improvement

Adapting to setbacks often requires seeing challenges as catalysts for growth. Instead of viewing failure as a roadblock, resilient investors recognize it as an opportunity to refine their processes, build stronger systems, and enhance their business model. For instance, an investor who encounters repeated cash flow issues may take this as a sign to implement more rigorous financial planning and budgeting processes. Similarly, an investor who struggles with tenant turnover might focus on improving tenant screening and property management practices to create a more stable, long-term rental environment.

Approaching challenges with a problem-solving mindset enables investors to identify the root causes of setbacks and address them systematically. Each difficulty becomes an opportunity to build a stronger, more adaptable business model. Whether it's improving due diligence, adjusting property management practices, or adopting a more conservative financing approach, investors who learn from challenges become better prepared for future investments.

Real estate developer Emily Tran describes how challenges have shaped her business: "Every setback is an opportunity to get better. If I notice a recurring problem—whether it's with budgeting, tenant management, or market timing—I take it as a chance to improve. Those lessons have made my business more resilient over time." By treating challenges as opportunities, investors not only refine their operations but also cultivate a resilient approach that will serve them well throughout their careers.

Building Strength Through Adaptability

Resilience and adaptability are essential qualities for long-term success in real estate. By reassessing goals, learning from feedback, and viewing challenges as opportunities for improvement, investors develop the flexibility to respond to changing circumstances. Embracing resilience allows investors to move forward with confidence, knowing that they can navigate setbacks and emerge stronger from each experience.

The real estate industry is full of variables that cannot be controlled, from market cycles to tenant behavior to economic shifts. Resilient investors focus on what they can control—their response to challenges, their willingness to learn, and their ability to adapt. With a resilient mindset, investors can face setbacks head-on, using each experience to build a stronger foundation for their future success.

Building a Risk Management Mindset

Real estate investing involves risk—it's a fact of the business. From fluctuating market conditions to unexpected property repairs, each investment carries the potential for challenges that can impact profitability. While risks can't be eliminated entirely, they can be managed. A proactive approach to risk management helps investors prepare for the unexpected, safeguard their portfolios, and build confidence in their decision-making. By developing a risk management mindset, investors learn to assess potential threats, implement mitigation strategies, and ensure their business can withstand inevitable setbacks.

Planning for Contingencies and Building Financial Buffers

Effective risk management begins with planning for contingencies. No matter how well an investment is researched, things can go wrong—renovations can run over budget, tenants may default on rent, or markets may experience sudden downturns. Planning for these scenarios means creating a financial cushion, such as a reserve fund, that can cover unexpected expenses without jeopardizing the investor's overall financial health. A general rule of thumb is to keep three to six months' worth of operating expenses in a reserve fund, but investors with larger portfolios or riskier projects may want to set aside more.

Contingency planning also involves building flexibility into project timelines and budgets. For example, when estimating renovation costs, adding a 10% to 20% buffer can accommodate unforeseen expenses. Similarly, allowing extra time for project completion helps account for potential delays, whether due to contractor availability, permit issues, or weather conditions. By anticipating these potential obstacles, investors can stay on track even when things don't go as planned.

Investor Susan Morales shares her approach: "Every project has unknowns, so I always build a cushion into my budget and timeline. Whether it's a longer project schedule or extra funds for unexpected repairs, those contingencies have saved me from stress—and from having to make rushed decisions." By planning for contingencies, investors can face setbacks with a clear head, knowing they have the resources to manage challenges without sacrificing their goals.

Assessing Risk Tolerance and Diversifying Investments

Understanding personal risk tolerance is crucial for developing a risk management strategy that aligns with an investor's goals and comfort level. Risk tolerance refers to an investor's ability and willingness to withstand potential losses. For example, some investors are comfortable taking on higher-risk investments, such as fix-and-flip projects or properties in volatile markets, in exchange for the potential of higher returns. Others may prefer stable, lower-risk investments, like long-term rental properties in established neighborhoods, which offer consistent cash flow with less exposure to market fluctuations.

Diversification is another key element of risk management. By spreading investments across different asset types, locations, and strategies, investors reduce the impact of any single property or market downturn on their overall portfolio. For example, a diversified portfolio may include a mix of residential rentals, commercial properties, and short-term rentals in different geographic areas. This approach balances higher-risk investments with more stable assets, providing a buffer against fluctuations in any one sector or location.

Investor James Patel highlights the importance of diversification: "Early on, I was heavily invested in one type of property in a single market. When that market took a hit, so did my portfolio. Now, I spread my investments out—different property types, different cities. It's not just about making money; it's about protecting what you've built." By assessing risk tolerance and diversifying investments, investors create a balanced portfolio that is better equipped to handle market shifts and unexpected challenges.

Implementing Risk Mitigation Strategies

Proactive risk mitigation involves identifying potential risks before they become problems and implementing strategies to minimize their impact. This might include conducting stress tests on cash flow projections to see how a property performs under different scenarios, such as increased vacancy rates or rising interest rates. Stress testing helps investors understand how sensitive their investments are to changes and allows them to plan accordingly, whether by building up reserves, adjusting rents, or restructuring financing.

Insurance is another vital component of risk mitigation. Investors should review their insurance policies regularly to ensure they have adequate coverage for property damage, liability, and business interruption. Specialized policies, such as flood or earthquake insurance, may be necessary depending on the location and specific risks associated with the property. In addition to traditional insurance, rental income insurance can provide coverage for lost income if a property becomes uninhabitable due to a covered loss.

Legal protections, such as forming an LLC (Limited Liability Company), can also help investors manage risk. An LLC separates personal assets from business liabilities, protecting the investor's personal wealth in the event of a lawsuit or significant financial loss. Working with attorneys, accountants, and insurance agents to develop a comprehensive risk management plan ensures that every potential threat is addressed and mitigated to the extent possible.

Property manager and investor Kate Jensen shares her approach to risk mitigation: "I run cash flow projections under different scenarios—what if I have a vacancy for three months? What if expenses go up? And I make sure my insurance covers all potential risks. Being prepared means fewer surprises and more peace of mind." By proactively identifying risks and implementing mitigation strategies, investors build resilience into their business and protect their assets against unforeseen events.

Navigating Real Estate with Confidence

Risk management is an ongoing process that evolves as an investor's portfolio grows and market conditions change. By planning for contingencies, understanding risk tolerance, diversifying investments, and implementing proactive risk mitigation strategies, investors can approach real estate with greater confidence and control. A solid risk management plan allows investors to pursue growth opportunities without exposing themselves to unnecessary risks, ensuring they can navigate challenges effectively and protect their long-term success.

The ability to manage risk is what separates successful investors from those who struggle when faced with setbacks. By building a risk management mindset, investors are better equipped to handle the ups and downs of the market, weather unexpected storms, and thrive in any economic environment. A disciplined approach to risk management provides the stability needed to pursue ambitious goals while minimizing the likelihood of costly setbacks, creating a foundation for sustainable growth in the real estate industry.

Chapter 24: Future Trends in Real Estate

The Rise of Technology and PropTech in Real Estate

Technology is rapidly transforming the real estate industry, driving new efficiencies, enhancing customer experiences, and reshaping traditional ways of doing business. PropTech, or property technology, encompasses a wide range of digital tools and platforms that simplify transactions, streamline property management, and optimize investment decisions. As these technologies continue to advance, they offer real estate investors, agents, and property managers powerful tools to stay competitive and increase the value they bring to their clients and tenants.

PropTech Innovations Transforming the Industry

One of the most notable advancements in real estate technology is the rise of virtual and augmented reality (VR/AR) in property tours. Virtual tours allow potential buyers and tenants to explore properties from anywhere in the world, providing an immersive experience without needing to step foot on-site.

This technology has proven especially valuable in residential and commercial real estate, where buyers often want to evaluate multiple options before making a decision. Virtual tours save time, reduce travel expenses, and make it easier for agents to show properties to a broader audience, streamlining the sales process.

Artificial intelligence (AI) and machine learning are also making significant strides in real estate. AI-driven platforms can analyze large volumes of data, identify market trends, and predict property values, helping investors make data-informed decisions. For property managers, AI is streamlining tenant relations and maintenance. Chatbots, for instance, can handle routine tenant inquiries, while AI-driven systems can schedule preventive maintenance based on predictive analytics, reducing downtime and prolonging the lifespan of building systems. These AI applications increase operational efficiency and provide tenants with faster, more reliable service, enhancing tenant satisfaction.

Blockchain technology is another game-changer, particularly in real estate transactions. Blockchain's decentralized and secure ledger system enables transparent, tamper-proof record-keeping, which can simplify property sales, title transfers, and leasing. Smart contracts—self-executing contracts coded into blockchain systems—ensure that all terms are met before a transaction is finalized, minimizing the risk of disputes and delays. This technology is especially promising in reducing fraud and providing secure transactions, appealing to international investors who seek secure, straightforward cross-border transactions.

Investor and technology advocate Sam Lister shares his view on blockchain's impact: "With blockchain, I can offer clients peace of mind by providing secure, transparent transactions. Smart contracts save time and reduce the legal complexities of traditional transactions, which is a huge advantage in a fast-paced market." By embracing blockchain, investors and agents can provide added security and efficiency to the transaction process, making it an attractive option for tech-savvy buyers and sellers.

Improving Customer Experience with Smart Home Technology

The integration of smart home technology has become increasingly popular as tenants and buyers seek convenience, security, and energy efficiency in their living spaces. Smart thermostats, lighting, and security systems allow residents to control their environment remotely, creating a personalized and user-friendly experience. These features not only appeal to tech-forward tenants but also contribute to energy savings by optimizing heating, cooling, and lighting based on occupancy. For property owners, installing smart systems can reduce utility costs, improve property value, and enhance tenant satisfaction.

For example, a property equipped with a smart thermostat can adjust temperature settings when a unit is unoccupied, saving energy without compromising comfort. Smart locks, which allow for keyless entry, also provide enhanced security and convenience for tenants, making it easier for property managers to handle unit access without needing to manage physical keys. Beyond convenience, these technologies are increasingly in demand among environmentally conscious tenants who value sustainable living solutions.

Property manager and investor Megan Ortiz highlights the benefits of smart home technology: "Tenants love the convenience of smart home features, and we see lower energy bills as a result. It's a win-win. The technology pays for itself over time and makes our properties stand out." By implementing smart home technology, investors not only attract tech-savvy tenants but also add value to their properties through cost savings and increased tenant appeal.

Optimizing Property Management with Data-Driven Tools

Data analytics has become an indispensable tool for property management, enabling property owners to make more informed decisions about marketing, tenant retention, and maintenance. Data-driven tools analyze tenant behavior, track occupancy trends, and monitor market conditions, allowing property managers to predict demand, set competitive rental prices, and make improvements that enhance tenant satisfaction. Advanced property management software platforms also offer features for tracking rental payments, managing leases, and communicating with tenants, making it easier to handle the complexities of managing multiple properties.

For example, predictive maintenance, driven by data analysis, allows property managers to identify when appliances, HVAC systems, or building structures may require maintenance before they fail. By addressing these needs proactively, property managers avoid costly emergency repairs, maintain property value, and ensure a comfortable environment for tenants. Additionally, data analytics can help identify high-value tenants, reducing vacancy rates by offering incentives or renewal options to tenants most likely to stay long-term.

Data analytics consultant and real estate advisor Jake Nguyen explains the value of data-driven management: "Data allows property managers to be proactive rather than reactive. Instead of waiting for issues to arise, they can anticipate and address them, which improves tenant retention and lowers costs. It's a powerful shift in how we manage properties." By using data-driven tools, property managers can optimize operations, reduce costs, and create a more stable income stream, which is crucial for sustainable growth.

Staying Competitive in a Tech-Driven Industry

The rise of PropTech is changing the face of real estate, offering a range of tools that improve efficiency, enhance customer experience, and streamline transactions. Investors, agents, and property managers who embrace these innovations are better positioned to meet the expectations of modern tenants and buyers, who increasingly value convenience, security, and transparency. From virtual tours and AI-driven analytics to blockchain and smart home technology, the PropTech revolution is opening new avenues for efficiency and growth in the real estate industry.

Adopting these technologies is not just about staying current; it's about building a future-ready real estate business that can adapt to changing market demands. By embracing PropTech, real estate professionals can enhance operational efficiency, reduce costs, and provide added value to clients and tenants. As technology continues to advance, those who leverage these tools will find themselves at the forefront of an evolving industry, equipped to meet the challenges and opportunities of tomorrow's real estate market.

The Shift Toward Sustainable and Eco-Friendly Developments

As environmental concerns grow, the real estate industry is experiencing a significant shift toward sustainable and eco-friendly practices. Investors, developers, and property managers are increasingly focusing on energy-efficient buildings, renewable materials, and sustainable design, both to meet regulatory demands and to appeal to eco-conscious tenants and buyers. Sustainability in real estate isn't just about reducing environmental impact; it also enhances property value, lowers operating costs, and supports long-term investment resilience. By adopting green building practices and aligning with sustainability trends, investors can future-proof their properties and create a positive impact.

The Benefits of Energy Efficiency and Renewable Resources

Energy efficiency has become a central pillar of sustainable real estate development. By incorporating energy-saving features such as efficient HVAC systems, LED lighting, and well-insulated building materials, property owners can significantly reduce their energy consumption, resulting in lower operating costs and reduced environmental impact. For example, a building with high-efficiency windows, advanced insulation, and a smart thermostat system can reduce heating and cooling costs by up to 30%, making it more cost-effective to operate over time. Such energy-efficient properties are also more attractive to tenants who prioritize sustainability and lower utility bills.

Renewable energy sources, like solar panels and geothermal heating, are becoming increasingly popular for both residential and commercial properties. Solar energy, in particular, offers numerous benefits: solar panels can provide a substantial portion of a building's electricity needs, reducing dependence on the grid and lowering energy costs. In some regions, government incentives, tax credits, and rebates for solar installations make renewable energy even more attractive for investors looking to improve their properties' sustainability without breaking the bank.

Developer and sustainability advocate Tom Jensen emphasizes the long-term benefits of energy efficiency: "Energy-efficient buildings don't just save money—they're also more resilient. A property that requires less energy is less vulnerable to rising utility costs, making it a stronger investment in the long run." By incorporating energy-efficient features and renewable energy sources, investors reduce operating costs and build properties that are better positioned to weather market and environmental changes.

Green Building Certifications and Standards

Green building certifications, such as LEED (Leadership in Energy and Environmental Design), WELL, and BREEAM, are gaining traction as property owners and developers aim to meet higher environmental and health standards. These certifications provide a recognized framework for assessing and improving a building's environmental performance, focusing on areas such as energy use, water efficiency, indoor air quality, and sustainable material sourcing. Properties with green certifications are often seen as more valuable, as they signal a commitment to sustainability that resonates with modern tenants and buyers.

LEED certification, for example, is one of the most widely recognized standards, with certification levels ranging from LEED Certified to LEED Platinum, depending on the property's environmental performance. A LEED-certified building is likely to have features such as low-flow water fixtures, energy-efficient lighting, and sustainable landscaping, which conserve resources and improve the property's overall environmental impact. The WELL certification, on the other hand, emphasizes occupant health and wellbeing, focusing on aspects like air quality, lighting, and access to green spaces.

Certified properties not only attract environmentally conscious tenants but also benefit from increased occupancy rates and potentially higher rental or sale prices. Many tenants and buyers are willing to pay a premium for spaces that align with their environmental values, especially in urban areas where sustainable living is a priority. Investor Lisa Murray explains, "Tenants are becoming more aware of the impact buildings have on the environment. By investing in certifications, we're not only contributing to a healthier planet but also appealing to a growing market segment that values sustainability." Green building certifications help investors and developers distinguish their properties and contribute to a future-focused brand image.

Sustainable Building Materials and Design

In addition to energy efficiency, the choice of building materials and design practices plays a crucial role in creating eco-friendly properties. Sustainable materials, such as recycled steel, reclaimed wood, and low-VOC (volatile organic compound) paints, help reduce a building's carbon footprint and minimize harmful emissions. For instance, reclaimed wood and recycled metal not only reduce the demand for new resources but also add unique aesthetic appeal, giving properties a distinctive character that appeals to environmentally conscious tenants.

Water conservation is another key aspect of sustainable design. Features like low-flow plumbing fixtures, rainwater harvesting systems, and drought-resistant landscaping reduce water usage, which is especially valuable in areas prone to water scarcity. These systems not only save on water costs but also support conservation efforts that are increasingly important in regions facing climate-related water challenges. Sustainable landscaping practices, such as using native plants and installing permeable paving, further enhance a property's eco-friendliness by reducing water runoff and supporting local ecosystems.

Architect and green building expert Sarah Rodriguez shares the impact of sustainable materials: "The materials you choose are just as important as the energy systems you install. Recycled and low-impact materials reduce environmental harm and create healthier indoor spaces for occupants. Plus, they align with the growing consumer demand for sustainable living." By using eco-friendly materials and sustainable design principles, developers create properties that are not only better for the environment but also more attractive to modern tenants and buyers.

Building a Sustainable Future in Real Estate

The shift toward sustainability in real estate reflects both consumer demand and an industry-wide recognition of the need for eco-friendly practices. As energy costs rise, natural resources become scarcer, and environmental awareness grows, properties that incorporate sustainable features are becoming increasingly valuable. Investors and developers who prioritize sustainability gain a competitive advantage, attracting tenants who value environmentally responsible living while reducing operational costs and enhancing property longevity.

Sustainable real estate is more than a trend—it's a lasting shift in how properties are designed, built, and operated. By embracing energy-efficient systems, green certifications, and sustainable materials, real estate professionals can align their investments with the future needs of the industry and the planet. As sustainable practices become the standard, those who commit to eco-friendly developments will be well-positioned for long-term success in an evolving market.

Adapting to Demographic Shifts and Changing Buyer Preferences

Demographic changes and evolving lifestyle preferences are reshaping the real estate landscape. As new generations enter the housing market, an aging population requires different types of housing, and remote work continues to influence where and how people choose to live. Understanding these shifts is crucial for investors, as aligning strategies with these trends can unlock opportunities in emerging markets and meet the needs of today's buyers and tenants. By adapting to demographic changes, real estate professionals can stay ahead of demand and create investments that resonate with modern preferences.

The Impact of Remote Work and Flexible Living Arrangements

One of the most transformative trends in recent years has been the rise of remote work, which has expanded the possibilities for where people live. Freed from the need to commute daily, many workers are seeking homes in suburban, rural, or even remote areas where property costs are lower, and quality of life may be higher. As a result, demand for single-family homes and properties with extra space for home offices has surged in suburban and rural areas. Properties with features like dedicated workspaces, high-speed internet, and access to outdoor space have become especially attractive, offering investors an opportunity to cater to the remote work lifestyle.

Additionally, some urban markets have seen a shift in rental demand, with young professionals seeking apartments that offer flexible spaces, co-working amenities, and common areas for collaboration and socializing. Buildings that offer amenities geared toward remote workers—such as shared office spaces, business centers, and high-speed internet infrastructure—are well-positioned to attract this demographic. This shift is encouraging developers to reimagine multifamily properties with layouts and amenities that cater to a blend of residential and work needs.

Real estate agent and market analyst Sarah Chen explains the appeal of remote-work-friendly properties: "Buyers are prioritizing homes that accommodate both work and living. Properties with home office space, outdoor areas, and flexible layouts are in high demand. Investors who recognize this shift can tap into a growing market." By designing or retrofitting properties to meet the needs of remote workers, investors can appeal to a lifestyle that is likely to persist well into the future.

Catering to an Aging Population with Senior-Friendly Housing

As the population ages, demand for senior-friendly housing is on the rise. Baby boomers, one of the largest demographic groups, are reaching retirement age and seeking housing options that accommodate their evolving needs. Many older adults are looking to downsize to smaller, more manageable homes or move into communities that offer medical support, social activities, and amenities designed for aging in place. Properties with features like single-level layouts, easy-to-navigate floor plans, and accessibility upgrades (such as grab bars and wider doorways) are increasingly appealing to this demographic.

Investors can also explore opportunities in age-restricted communities or senior living developments that offer specialized services for older adults. These communities often include healthcare facilities, fitness centers, and organized activities, creating a supportive environment that encourages both independence and social engagement. The demand for such properties is expected to grow as more baby boomers seek housing that provides a balance of independence and support, making senior-friendly developments a potentially lucrative investment.

Developer and senior housing specialist Michael Rogers emphasizes the importance of catering to older adults: "The senior population is growing, and they want homes that make life easier and safer. Features like single-story living, accessible bathrooms, and community amenities are key. For investors, this means a growing market that values these considerations." By understanding and responding to the needs of an aging population, investors can create properties that serve an essential market segment while enhancing community impact.

Addressing the Demand for Multi-Generational and Multi-Use Properties

As housing costs rise and family dynamics evolve, there is an increasing trend toward multi-generational living, where families share a home to pool resources and support each other. Properties designed for multi-generational living typically include multiple bedrooms, separate entrances, or auxiliary dwelling units (ADUs) that provide privacy while fostering a shared family environment. ADUs, in particular, have gained popularity as they allow extended families to live together while maintaining autonomy, providing both financial and social benefits.

Additionally, buyers and tenants are showing a growing interest in multi-use properties that can adapt to changing needs. For example, a property with a detached garage that can be converted into an office or rental unit, or a home with a basement suite that can serve as a rental or guest space, appeals to buyers looking for flexibility. These properties offer the potential for rental income, making them attractive to those interested in house hacking—living in one part of a property while renting out another to offset costs.

Investor and property manager Julia Lin highlights the value of multi-use properties: "People want homes that can adapt to their needs, whether it's space for parents, a rental unit, or a home office. Properties with flexible layouts or ADUs offer so much versatility, which really appeals to today's buyers." By investing in or developing properties that offer this flexibility, real estate professionals can cater to a range of buyer preferences, enhancing property appeal and creating diversified income opportunities.

Positioning for Success in a Changing Demographic Landscape

Demographic shifts and changing lifestyle preferences are reshaping demand across the real estate market. By understanding the impact of remote work, the needs of an aging population, and the desire for multi-generational and multi-use properties, investors can make strategic decisions that align with these trends. Tailoring properties to meet the preferences of today's buyers and tenants not only enhances market appeal but also future-proofs investments as these trends continue to evolve.

The ability to adapt to demographic shifts provides a competitive advantage, ensuring that properties remain relevant and in demand. Investors who recognize and respond to these trends position themselves to create value in both the short and long term, meeting the needs of diverse audiences and aligning their portfolios with the future of real estate. By embracing these demographic changes, real estate professionals can build resilient, versatile investments that cater to the evolving lifestyles of modern buyers and tenants.

Conclusion: Building Your Own Path in Real Estate

The journey through real estate is both challenging and rewarding, filled with opportunities to grow, adapt, and build something meaningful. Whether you're just starting out or you've built a substantial portfolio, each lesson, every success, and even the occasional setback contribute to shaping your unique path. The insights and strategies shared throughout this book—from understanding market fundamentals and leveraging new technologies to embracing sustainable practices and adapting to demographic shifts—are tools to guide you as you navigate the industry. Implementing these principles, however, will require a commitment to discovery, self-reflection, and ongoing learning.

Real estate offers infinite ways to succeed, but success is rarely a one-size-fits-all formula. The most impactful strategies are the ones that align with your personal goals, values, and circumstances. Finding your unique approach means taking time to reflect on what excites you about real estate and recognizing the strengths you bring to the table. Whether you are drawn to rental properties, development projects, or innovative PropTech solutions, leaning into your interests and strengths will help you create a path that's both fulfilling and profitable.

At its core, real estate is an industry that rewards lifelong learners. Markets change, technologies evolve, and buyer preferences shift, making adaptability a crucial skill. Stay curious, embrace new ideas, and don't hesitate to refine your strategy as you grow. Continuing education, mentorship, and a willingness to learn from both wins and setbacks will keep you resilient and capable of navigating any real estate cycle.

As you move forward, remember that every investor's journey is different. The insights from industry leaders and real-world examples shared in this book are here to provide you with guidance, but ultimately, the path you forge will be your own. With a solid foundation, a growth mindset, and a commitment to constant improvement, you are well-prepared to build a legacy in real estate that reflects your vision and values.

Your journey is yours to shape—embrace it with confidence, perseverance, and a passion for what lies ahead. Here's to your success in building your own path in real estate.